BOAT GREEN

Boat green? Here's 50 steps boaters can take to start to save the waters. In this mixed-up world, maybe we can get our fellow humans to start thinking about the future by taking them out on the water. Let's share our experiences — and maybe there'll be a human race here in 100 years.

— Pete Seeger, Folksinger, Activist.

Boat Green is a highly welcome book for boaters, written by a boater. It's pragmatic, practical and well researched, yet at the same time inspiring and supportive to the challenges facing boaters. Overall, a terrific resource for boaters who want to leave a "green wake" — and in reality, it's a book that every boat owner, vessel operator and crewmember should read.

— Mike Richards, Program Coordinator, Green Boating, Georgia Strait Alliance.

Comprehensive, accurate and practical, this book is a great step forward on how to minimize your boating impact on the environment while maximizing awareness, good practice and enjoyment. Thanks, Clyde, for leading the way!

— Don Douglass & Réanne Hemingway-Douglass, Explorers and Authors of the *Exploring Series* guidebooks and detailed Cruising Maps covering the West Coast from Baja California to the Gulf of Alaska

Enjoying the beauty and tranquility of a quiet anchorage,
we often ponder the natural world around us, the birds, the
trees along the shoreline, and the sea creatures that swirl beneath
the surface. And our presence makes us part of this world.
Author Clyde Ford blends history, science, and spiritual discovery
to help us learn to live in closer harmony with our watery planet.
Recognizing the finite resources around us and the impact
we have on our boats, his views can enlighten the boating
community to better support a more green approach to boating.
In so many ways, it is an important shift in thinking as
we come to grips with a natural world in crisis.

— Bill Parlatore, Editor-in-Chief *PassageMaker Magazine*

BOAT GREEN

50 Steps Boaters Can Take to Save Our Waters

CLYDE W. FORD

NEW SOCIETY PUBLISHERS

CATALOGING IN PUBLICATION DATA
A catalog record for this publication is available from the
National Library of Canada.

Cover design by Diane McIntosh.
Photos: Getty/Alamy/iStock.

Printed in Canada.
First printing January 2008.

Paperback ISBN: 978-0-86571-590-5

Inquiries regarding requests to reprint all or part of *Boat Green* should
be addressed to New Society Publishers at the address below.

To order directly from the publishers, please call toll-free (North America)
1-800-567-6772, or order online at www.newsociety.com

Any other inquiries can be directed by mail to:

New Society Publishers
P.O. Box 189, Gabriola Island, BC V0R 1X0, Canada
(250) 247-9737

New Society Publishers' mission is to publish books that contribute in funda-
mental ways to building an ecologically sustainable and just society, and to do
so with the least possible impact on the environment, in a manner that models
this vision. We are committed to doing this not just through education, but
through action. This book is one step toward ending global deforestation and
climate change. It is printed on acid-free paper that is 100% **post-consumer
recycled** (100% old growth forest-free), processed chlorine free, and printed
with vegetable-based, low-VOC inks, with covers produced using Forest
Stewardship Council-certified stock. Additionally, New Society purchases carbon
offsets based on an annual emissions audit, operating with a carbon-neutral
footprint. For further information, or to browse our full list of books and purchase securely, visit our website at: www.newsociety.com

NEW SOCIETY PUBLISHERS   www.newsociety.com

Contents

Acknowledgments

Mike Richards and Scott Blake for reading and commenting on early versions of the manuscript. Judith Brand, my editor. EJ Hurst, my publicist. Judith and Christoper Plant, MJ Jessen, Diane McIntosh, Ingrid Witvoet, Sue Custance and the staff of New Society for their vision and commitment to making a difference. And most of all to the love of my life, Chara Stuart, for her perseverance and belief in me.

A Note on the Chapter Icons

At the head of each chapter you will find a series of one to four icons that give an indication of which aspects of boating and the marine environment are dealt with. The icons have the following meanings:

 Related to the health and safety of crew and vessel

 Related to vessel operation and maintenance

 Related to the enjoyment of boating and the marine environment

 Related to the protection of our waters and the marine environment

These icons are meant to be guides rather than definitive descriptors of the material in each chapter. Many times the categories represented by these icons overlap each other.

Dedication

To Pete Seeger for showing us that
boats and boaters can save our waters.

FOR YOURSELF

CHAPTER 1

How to Use This Book

Understand issues. Develop solutions. Take action.

M ariners are by nature practical. We often find ourselves in situations where we must assess conditions, assimilate information and take decisive action. We might be caught in a sudden gale under too much sail, or facing the transit of rapids that have turned sooner than expected. We haven't the luxury of theorizing about the meteorology of the storm because we need to pull in sail. And we haven't time to contemplate the hydrodynamics of the rapids because we must read the water and find back eddies to help us make headway through them. Meditation on our fate, our luck and the wisdom of our decisions can wait until we've made safe harbor.

Similarly, this is a practical book. There's no speculating about environmental theories or choosing sides over which arguments and facts are most believable when in comes to global warming and its effects. This book offers mariners practical information about enhancing vessel performance, decreasing operating costs, improving the safety of vessel and crew and deriving greater enjoyment from being on the water, with the added benefit of protecting the marine environment and minimizing the impact of recreational boating on our lakes, streams, rivers and oceans.

Each chapter begins with a short summary of a particular issue or topic. That is followed by the concise presentation of information about that topic or issue, most often in the form of bulleted items. Sections entitled Steps You Can Take list specific steps that you can take in regard to the subject matter of the chapter. Not every step will be applicable to you and your boat. Select the steps you need or want to take.

Toward the end of the chapter you'll find various sources: reading material and website references. Endnotes to material cited appear at the back of the book. Most chapters end with Internet Search Terms. With so much reliance on the Internet to find information, I thought it important to include this section of terms according to familiar searching rules used on popular sites such as Google. Each term is separated by a semi-colon, and related words are enclosed in quotes so the search engine will look for them together.

The Internet, however, is such a dynamic environment that Web addresses (URLs) that are valid one day are often invalid the next. So be sure you use each Web reference in the book as a guide. Be prepared that occasionally you will attempt to navigate to a location given in the book that no longer exists.

Steps You Can Take

- Read the book as a whole from cover to cover.
- Mark the chapters or items that peak your interest.
- Take everything you read as the first word on a subject, not the last word.
- Use the reference sources to learn more.
- Consider carefully what steps you'd like to take.
- If any steps involve making changes to mechanical or electrical equipment on your boat, be sure you are comfortable doing that yourself. If not, hire a professional shipwright or boat mechanic.
- Don't try to take every step listed in this book. It wasn't written for that purpose. Find a step or a handful of steps that appeal to you. Those are the steps you should take.
- Keep a log of the steps you make in the form of a written log, a journal or even a set of photographs.
- Once you've had some time to evaluate the success of taking one step suggested in this book, let others know about your experience. See chapter 50 for more on this.
- Once you've taken and completed your first "boat green" step, plan your next.
- And remember, the ultimate point of *Boat Green* is to enjoy boating while protecting the waters we boat on.

Resource

Ecomarine Institute: www.ecomarine.org. See the latest updates on boating and the marine environment, leave your questions and comments and interact with other boaters in the forum area.

Internet Search Terms

"boat green"; boating "marine environment" protection; "clean boating"; "green boating"

CHAPTER 2

What Does It Mean to Boat Green?

A way. A commitment. A desire to make a difference.

B oat green is a way of boating that seeks to address the declining health of our oceans, rivers and lakes by recognizing that boaters, while not a major cause of marine environmental degradation, can be an important part of the solution. Boat green is a way of operating and maintaining a vessel that recognizes and protects the value of our offshore, coastal and inland waters along with their associated ecosystems. Boat green contributes to the health and safety of a vessel operator and crew and to other vessels and crews. Boat green improves vessel performance and reduces vessel maintenance, often resulting in lower overall costs of owning a vessel. And boat green enhances the enjoyment of being on the water.

The Value of the Marine Environment

How do you value the marine environment in which we boat? Often we think of value in economic terms by asking: What is this worth to me? So, let me ask that question: What is the marine environment worth to you? If you're not a commercial fisherman, tugboat operator, tanker crew member or someone who makes a living on the water, that question is not an easy one to answer. Most boaters spend more on the purchase, operation and maintenance of their boats than they will ever receive back in economic terms. Let's face it, it makes more economic sense to purchase fish from a local supermarket than to spend hundreds of thousands of dollars on the purchase of a vessel and then thousands of dollars operating and maintaining that vessel just to go fishing for a few weeks each year. And yet boaters do just that. Many don't even fish while they're on the water. So what then *is* the value of the marine environment?

Boat green begins with a recognition that the value of the marine environment lies beyond traditional economics. How do you place a monetary value on viewing a sunset from a secluded cove? Sailing on a broad reach with an expansive view of the coastline to port? Paddling an inlet and suddenly finding yourself in the midst of a pod of whales? Or waking up to the smell of salt air and gentle waves? You might find some way of assigning value to these experiences: they bring relief from the daily stresses of life and therefore reduce your need for psychotherapy or drugs; they enhance your productivity and creativity once you return to work after spending time in the marine environment. But such attempts at assigning value miss the point that the marine environment offers us values not easily quantifiable in economic terms — esthetic, emotional and spiritual values that are vitally important to us.

Take a moment to consider the value you derive from boating. Using the following list, check off which values apply to you.

- ❏ Beauty of being in the marine environment.
- ❏ Enjoyment of solitude.
- ❏ Release of stress.
- ❏ Opportunity to meet other like-minded boaters.
- ❏ Just cruising with no particular aim, destination or purpose.
- ❏ Joy of fishing.
- ❏ Beach-walking.
- ❏ Recreational activities done from your boat like snorkeling, scuba diving or kayaking.
- ❏ The spirituality of being on the water and in nature.
- ❏ Opportunity to see wildlife.
- ❏ Boating as a way of life.
- ❏ Ability to visit new places and people.
- ❏ Challenge of operating and maintaining a vessel.
- ❏ Joy and challenge of navigating.
- ❏ Thrill of adventure.
- ❏ Food tastes better when cooked from a boat.

Think of some more values of your own.

How important is it to you to preserve these values that you derive from being on the water? Based on the items you checked, how would you answer this question? There are no right or wrong answers because each person values the marine environment differently.

❑ Very Important. It would significantly diminish the quality of my life if I could not derive these values from the marine environment.

❑ Somewhat Important. It would impact my quality of life somewhat if I could not derive these values from the marine environment.

❑ Not Important. It would not impact my quality of life if I could not derive these values from the marine environment.

Are you willing to take steps to preserve the value you derive from the marine environment?

In some ways this is a trick question. Simply being a boater suggests your answer to this question is yes, because all boaters are subject to a number of laws, regulations and rules that help to preserve the marine environment. The basic coast guard safety regulations (see chapter 7) that all boaters are required to comply with not only enhance safety but also protect and preserve the marine environment. Similarly, the nautical Rules of the Road that we follow play an important role in safety and in environmental protection. You may keep your boat in a marina that has guidelines you must follow, and those guidelines often include protections for the marine environment.

In this respect, all boaters boat green by complying with these basic laws and regulations. This book simply builds upon what we already do as boaters by presenting and describing a number of additional steps that we can take to help preserve the marine environment from which we derive such important value in our lives.

Did You Know?

According to a 2006 survey conducted by Discover Boating and Russell Research, boaters turn to the water for peace and relaxation; 93 percent of boaters said their favorite hobby was a source of stress relief.[1] The survey uncovered more good news for boaters, as it seems the calming benefits of time spent on a boat continue while on land. Boaters expressed greater satisfaction with many quality of life aspects, including their physical fitness, health, love lives and performance of their children in school.

The survey, which polled more than 1,000 boaters and non-boaters, found that the perks of boating extend beyond the docks. Boaters expressed greater satisfaction with their physical fitness and overall health, as well as those of their children. The number of outdoor activities boaters enjoy once they set sail, such as fishing, scuba diving and wake boarding, may be one reason why boaters are more pleased with their active lifestyles than those who remain landlocked.

CHAPTER 3

The Health of Our Oceans

Worldwide, our oceans are in danger.

Have you ever cruised on a sun-drenched day, operating your boat from outside, when suddenly there's a puff of air, and as if by magic the arched backs of a school of dolphins emerge from the surrounding waters. For the next half hour, they ride your bow wave, crisscross just in front of you or leap high, pirouetting and flipping in mid-air like a troupe of aquatic ballerinas before disappearing below the surface again. Perhaps you've seen a humpback whale raise its dorsal fin, then tumble over on its side and travel with you, whale eye staring at human eye, as though communicating in a language beyond sound that seems to say, "I am a master of this watery realm, and I wish to know who visits my domain in such a fragile craft."

Perhaps you've watched a bald eagle screaming down from high above, striking the water like an airborne torpedo then struggling to rise again with a huge salmon snared in its talons. Maybe you have a favorite crabbing or prawning spot, where you can drop a trap, wait a few hours and then haul in enough food for several days. What about that fishing hole you know? The place where a stream meets the ocean and fish congregate like revelers on Mardi Gras. It seems a guilty pleasure. With every drop of your line, there's a bite and food to freeze for months to come.

Do you have favorite anchorage? An out-of-the-way spot fewer boaters know about; a place where you can "drop the hook" and for days you might not see another boat; a place where all you want to do is sit and stare out at the beauty around you, while you let the stress of your everyday life drain away.

Idyllic? Yes, but it's one reason that many of us boat.

Now imagine a cruise over your favorite grounds. No dolphins or whales break the water's surface. No fish jump. No eagles dive. No crabs and prawns climb into your traps. Or imagine arriving at your favorite anchorage only to find the stench of human waste so awful, you can't stomach staying for more than a few sad minutes before moving on.

Our oceans are dying. Dead zones like these are cropping up in off-shore and nearshore waters worldwide. This isn't meant to be a scare tactic, it's a simple statement of fact supported by decades of research, the observation of boaters and the demise of communities and liveli-hoods once based on the bounty of the sea.

The statistics are dismal, but they are also necessary to confront if as humans we wish to continue enjoying the splendor of the oceans for generations to come. As a boater, I've cruised over dying seas, and it brought me to tears. The experience also called me to action, searching for something — anything — that I could do, that would at least slow down the rate of decline of our oceans and perhaps give nature time to heal. Most of this book is about the steps we can take to prevent fur-ther damage to our oceans, but before we get there, we need to know the current poor health of our oceans.

Did You Know?

- Dissolved oxygen is critical to the life of most marine organisms.
- Dead zones are areas of the ocean where the bottom water has no or little oxygen.
- Eutrophication (which means "too many nutrients"), the process by which dead zones are created, is fairly simple:

  1. Plankton, and other aquatic plants, at the surface of the oceans die, producing organic matter which sinks to the bottom.
  2. Bacteria at the bottom of the oceans break down the organic matter.
  3. Plankton need sunlight and nutrients to survive. They take in carbon dioxide and produce oxygen during their lifetime.

4. Bacteria, on the other hand, take in the oxygen from the water and produce carbon dioxide as they feed on the organic matter from the plankton and break it down.

5. As bacteria remove oxygen from the water, there is none left for the marine life that depends on it for survival.

6. When plankton colonies grow very large they overwhelm the bacteria that normally breaks down organic matter.

7. Dead zones are the result.

- Human pollutants, particularly from agricultural runoff, finds its way into streams and rivers and ultimately into the oceans where those runoffs provide food for the plankton, escalating the cycle of depleting oxygen.

- Many dead zones begin around the mouths of river systems, like the Mississippi, and then spread offshore, a process known as "creeping dead zones."

- Large blooms of plankton also restrict water flow, which in turn prevents normal ocean tides and currents from refreshing oxygen-depleted waters with oxygen-rich waters.

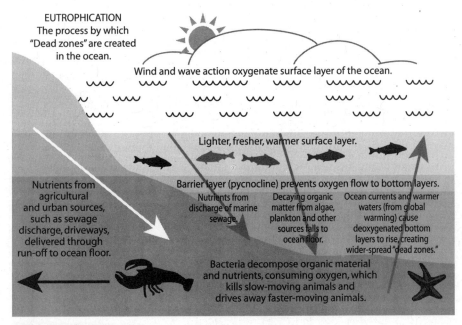

Fig. 3.1: *Eutrophication.*

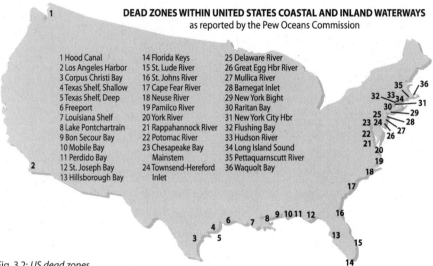

DEAD ZONES WITHIN UNITED STATES COASTAL AND INLAND WATERWAYS
as reported by the Pew Oceans Commission

1 Hood Canal	14 Florida Keys	25 Delaware River
2 Los Angeles Harbor	15 St. Lude River	26 Great Egg Hbr River
3 Corpus Christi Bay	16 St. Johns River	27 Mullica River
4 Texas Shelf, Shallow	17 Cape Fear River	28 Barnegat Inlet
5 Texas Shelf, Deep	18 Neuse River	29 New York Bight
6 Freeport	19 Pamilco River	30 Raritan Bay
7 Louisiana Shelf	20 York River	31 New York City Hbr
8 Lake Pontchartrain	21 Rappahannock River	32 Flushing Bay
9 Bon Secour Bay	22 Potomac River	33 Hudson River
10 Mobile Bay	23 Chesapeake Bay	34 Long Island Sound
11 Perdido Bay	Mainstem	35 Pettaquarnscutt River
12 St. Joseph Bay	24 Townsend-Hereford	36 Waquolt Bay
13 Hillsborough Bay	Inlet	

Fig. 3.2: *US dead zones*

- Any pollutants that cause an increase in plankton blooms can contribute to this problem.
- Cruise ships that regularly dump raw sewage into harbors may contribute to the creation of mini dead zones.
- Many recreational boaters who discharge their heads in areas of low tidal exchange can also assist in the creation of mini dead zones. Human sewage is a good source of nutrients for aquatic plants.

In 2003 the Pew Oceans Commission released a major report on the state of the oceans entitled "America's Living Oceans."[1] Its findings were stark and often grim:

- The amount of oil running off our streets and driveways and ultimately flowing into the oceans is equal to an *Exxon Valdez* oil spill — 10.9 million gallons — every eight months.
- The amount of nitrogen released into coastal waters along the Atlantic seaboard and the Gulf of Mexico from human activity such as fertilizers and livestock sewage has increased about fivefold since the pre-industrial era, and may increase another 30 percent by 2030 if current practices continue.
- Two-thirds of our estuaries and bays are either moderately or severely degraded by areas of spreading dead zones.

- More than 13,000 beaches were closed or under pollution advisories in 2001, an increase of 20 percent from the previous year.

Human Health and Ocean Health Are Linked

The oceans give us life: 50% to 70% of the oxygen we breathe comes from oxygen produced by aquatic plants and organisms. Oceans cover 70% of the Earth's surface, and 60% of the human population lives on or near the coastline, including more than 50% of the United States population. Human pollution of the oceans supports the rise of toxic algal blooms worldwide, which in turn move up the food chain in marine organisms such as shellfish. When eaten by humans, these produce symptoms that include nausea, respiratory problems and memory loss; fatality rates exceed 10% in some cases.[2]

Human-assisted climate change (global warming) results is higher ocean temperatures, which in turn can cause seawater to carry deadly human pathogens like cholera.[3] As the oceans become barren, human nutrition suffers. More than two billion people worldwide depend on the oceans for a substantial source of their daily protein. We have already harvested more than 90% of the large fish that live on continental shelves and the open water.[4] For the time being, affluent nations feel little impact from the decline of the sea as a source of food, but the populations of poorer developing nations are suffering from empty nets and contaminated catches pulled from the sea. In 2004 the United States Congress passed the Oceans and Human Health Act, to further study this issue.

Hope Amidst Gloom

As dismal as the reports on the health of oceans are, one can still find hope. Almost fished to extinction in the 1970s, striped bass, or rock fish, have made a dramatic comeback along the Atlantic seaboard in the last two decades through strict limits on fishing and a concerted restocking effort by federal and state governments. Restocking and a "zero-catch" policy have led to surprisingly large stocks of Eastern sturgeon in the Hudson River and other eastern seaboard estuaries. In 1997 North Atlantic swordfish had been fished to the brink of extinction. "Give the Swordfish a Break," a campaign spearheaded by the National Resources Defense Council (NRDC) and Washington, DC restaurateur Nora Pouillon, led to strict limits on catches and closure of fishing for swordfish in breeding grounds. In 2000 NRDC ended its campaign, with swordfish stock recovering to nearly 94% of what biologists considered a healthy, sustainable level.

After Los Angeles reduced waste discharges into nearby waters, kelp beds, seabirds and fish stocks returned to coastal waters.

Recreational boating and fishing are not major contributors to the decline of our nation's coastal and offshore waters. But the actions of recreational boaters can be a major force in demonstrating to others the importance of caring for the marine environment that we boaters treasure. Yes, our oceans are ailing. But by scrupulously taking actions and making boating decisions that reduce pollution and minimize harm to the marine environment, we can give our oceans a chance to heal.

Internet Search Terms

"Pew Oceans Commission"; eutrophication; "dead zones" ocean; "striped bass" comeback; sturgeon comeback; "North Atlantic swordfish" comeback

CHAPTER 4

The Health of Our Wetlands, Rivers, Streams and Lakes

Our inland water affects our oceans.

The mighty Mississippi River has humble beginnings in a scribble of lakes in Itasca, Minnesota. What takes place here and in the surrounding marshes and wetlands; what takes place along the numerous rivers and streams that feed Old Man River has a significant effect not only on the river but on the ocean it eventually empties into some 2,500 miles away. Likewise, our concerns and actions to preserve the marine environment should focus not only on the grand horizons of the oceans but also on the humble vista of our rivers, streams, lakes and wetlands. In fact, many boaters spend most of their boating life in freshwater, cruising and fishing on rivers and lakes. So, it behooves us to understand the role and importance of these inland waters to the health of the marine environment.

Wetlands

Wetlands, the "interface zones" between purely land-based environments and purely aquatic environments, provide shelter and food to diverse species. Leaves and stems break down in the water, providing food for insects, shellfish and forage fish, and nutrients for wetlands plants and algae. Fish, mammals, reptiles and amphibians eat aquatic invertebrates and forage for food in wetlands.

Wetlands are among the most biologically productive natural ecosystems in the world, comparable only to tropical rain forests and coral reefs in the diversity of species they support. They are vital to the survival of various animals and plants, including threatened and endangered species like the wood stork, Florida panther and whooping crane. The US Fish and Wildlife Service estimates that up to 43% of the threatened and endangered species rely directly or indirectly on wetlands for their survival. For many other species, such as the wood duck, muskrat and swamp rose, wetlands are primary habitats. For other species, wetlands provide important seasonal habitats where food, water and cover are plentiful.

Wetlands furnish a wealth of natural products, including fish, timber, wild rice and furs. For example, in the Southeast, 96% of the commercial catch and over 50% of the recreational harvest are fish and shellfish that depend on the estuary and coastal wetlands system. Waterfowl hunters spend over $600 million annually in pursuit of wetlands-dependent birds.

Wetlands often function like natural tubs or sponges, storing water (floodwater, or surface water that collects in isolated depressions) and slowly releasing it. Trees and other wetland vegetation help slow floodwaters. This combined action of storage and slowing can lower flood heights and reduce both the water's erosive potential, coastal or inland, and the likelihood of flood damage to crops. They also help to control increases in the rate and volume of runoff in urban areas.

Wetlands help improve water quality, including that of drinking water, by intercepting surface runoff and removing or retaining its nutrients, processing organic wastes, and reducing sediment before it reaches open water. By storing carbon within their plant communities and soil instead of releasing it to the atmosphere as carbon dioxide, wetlands help to moderate global climate conditions.

Wetlands provide opportunities for popular activities such as hiking, fishing and boating. For example, an estimated 50 million people spend approximately $10 billion each year observing and photographing wetlands-dependent birds.

Approximately 220 million acres of wetlands existed in the contiguous United States before the 1700s; less than 100 million acres of wetlands exist today. Each year 70,000 to 90,000 acres are lost due to human activities such as:

- Drainage
- Dredging and stream channelization
- Depositing fill material
- Dyking and damming
- Tilling for crop production
- Levees
- Logging
- Construction
- Mining
- Runoff
- Air and water pollutants
- Changing nutrient levels
- Releasing toxic chemicals
- Introducing non-native species
- Grazing by domestic animals[1]

Rivers, Streams and Lakes

Lakes and small streams are subject to many of the same man-made and natural processes. Four of the most important processes that affect the health of these bodies of water are:

Eutrophication

We have already discussed this universal threat to the health of off-shore, coastal and inland waters that produces dead zones. For lakes, however, eutrophication is a natural process that over hundreds of thousands of years can cause a lake to become a marsh or a bog, resembling a wetland. Human activity can accelerate this process, turning a healthy lake into an unhealthy bog in a generation. Runoffs from agricultural areas, cities, industrial wastewater and even recreational activities such as boating contribute to elevated nutrients in lakes and thus to the process of eutrophication.

Sedimentation

Wind and rain normally move soil from higher elevations down to lakes and small streams. Again, this is a natural evolutionary activity. But when humans clear land of trees and plants that hold down topsoil, the rate of sedimentation increases dramatically, causing lakes and small streams to fill-in.

Acidification

When air pollution from power plants, factories and cars mixes with moisture in clouds, a toxic brew is created that falls to earth and into lakes as acid rain. Thousands of lakes throughout North America are now too acidic to support fish and other aquatic life.

Toxic Contamination

Heavy metals from industrial runoff, pesticides, raw human waste funneled directly through municipal sewage pipes and airborne pollutants are just some of the contaminants that make their way into our lakes and streams. All forms of human disease organisms have been found in the nation's waters.

Sewer Systems

Sanitary Sewer Overflow, or SSO, is one prime contributor to the degradation of lakes and streams. SSO usually occurs when municipal sewer pipes overflow due to heavy rains. But aging sewer systems in many large cities are unable to handle the volume of human waste flowing through them, and so they are in a near-perpetual state of overflow. Dozens of cities like Cincinnati, some with sewer pipes laid in the 1800s, are dumping raw human waste into streams and lakes, a practice that is generally illegal under the 1972 Clean Water Act. Yet it continues an estimated 40,000 times every year because cities balk at the enormous expense of modernizing and expanding their sewage systems.[2]

Raw sewage in the water is a primary factor in the sickening of one million people a year, according to the Centers for Disease Control and Prevention.[3] Since 1996 Baltimore has dumped at least 100 million gallons of untreated waste into its waters. Some of the sewage spewed into tributaries of the Chesapeake Bay, one of the nation's top sources of shellfish.[4]

In December 2006 the US Environmental Protection Agency (US EPA) concluded a multi-year study on the health of America's small streams entitled "Wadeable Streams Assessment."[5] Using small invertebrates like insect larvae, snails, crayfish and worms as "indicator species," the study concluded that:

- 28% of US stream miles were in good condition compared to the best available reference sites in their regions, 25% were in fair condition and 42% were in poor condition. Another 5% were not assessed.
- Eutrophication (see page 11) and sediment pollution from human activities such as farming and construction were among the top causes of degraded stream quality.
- Increased salinity from irrigation and water withdrawal for other

uses also degraded the quality of streams.

- Increased acidity was found in the nation's streams from nearby industrial activities such as mining for coal.

The EPA is undertaking a major three-year study of the health of the nation's lakes, begun in 2007.

Caring for our nation's waterways begins at home. What leaves our houses can find its way into our lakes, streams, rivers and ultimately our oceans. As mariners, who value pristine anchorages offshore, we must also ensure that cleaner water finds its way into our lakes, streams and rivers.

Steps You Can Take

- Learn more about the health of your local lakes, streams and rivers.
- Advocate for legislation that promotes reduction of human sewage dumping into our feeder waterways, reduction of pollution discharges and reduction of agricultural runoffs.
- Don't fill in wetlands on your property, build inland.
- Be a pooper scooper and pick-up after your pets.
- Keep pets and livestock out of lakes, streams and rivers.
- If you notice oil, gas or other fluid spots where you park your car, have your car serviced.
- If you apply fertilizer and chemicals to your lawn, follow the application instructions found on the label.
- Store and dispose of household chemicals properly. Always use them in the way they were intended. Seal the product to prevent leakage and to preserve it for later use. Take unwanted hazardous wastes to a proper disposal site.
- Keep storm drains and street gutters clear of debris. Bag or mulch lawn clippings so they don't blow into the street.
- If you boat on a lake or river, follow the applicable guidelines and practices described in this book.
- **Remember:** What happens upstream affects the waters we treasure downstream.

Internet Search Terms

"lake health"; "stream health"; "river health"; "urban runoff"; "industrial runoff"; "acid rain"; wetlands; eutrophication

CHaPTeR 5

Boat Green and Global Warming

Mariners should "keep a weather eye" on global warming.

Is Global Warming Really Happening?

Some people believe that global warming is a myth, a falsehood perpetrated by environmentalist conspirators to alarm people and force them to radically alter the lifestyles they have come to know and enjoy. Others point to any and every shift in a weather pattern or the occurrence of a natural disaster as evidence that "global warming" is not only real, but that we are already deep within its clutches and doomed. What both extremes have in common is their distance from a set of facts or truth about "global warming."

In 2005 the US National Academy of Sciences, along with academies of sciences from ten other nations, issued an unequivocal statement about global warming and its effects (see IPCC statement at the end of this chapter) that made it clear that *the only debate over global warming in the scientific community concerns how much and how fast warming will continue as a result of human activity*. These scientists gave a pointed, concise warning about global warming — its causes and its solutions — and asked world leaders to implement solutions immediately.

Of course, it's still possible to dismiss these world-renowned academies and the scientists they represent as doing "junk science," or castigate them for "not doing enough." The point of this chapter, and this book, is not to take sides in the debate about whether global warming is really happening and whether we are doing enough to respond. Anyone who's

21

interested can read the facts from both sides of this debate and make up their own mind. The point of this chapter is to promote being a "prudent mariner" with regard to global warming.

Have you ever listened to your weather radio early one morning just before you're about to cast off? Perhaps the weather forecaster says, "A low pressure system is moving in over the forecast area, bringing with it southerly gales of 30 to 40 knots later today and early tomorrow." What would you do? Some boaters will simply stay in port. Other boaters will say, "The hell with the forecast, they're always wrong anyway." While the prudent mariner will listen to the forecast, evaluate the risks and perhaps then set out but always "keeping a weather eye," as the old nautical phrase goes. "Keeping a weather eye" doesn't simply mean checking the sky every two minutes to see if it has grown dark. It means evaluating sea conditions and boat and crew readiness and making plans and taking preparatory actions in the event the storm does strike, perhaps sooner or more severely than predicted. I believe that as mariners we should "keep a weather eye" to global warming, making plans and taking prudent actions in the event that it does strike sooner and more severely than predicted.

Global Warming and the Health of Our Waters

There are two major ways to look at the relationship of global warming to the health of the marine environment. First, the human activities giving rise to global warming are the same activities giving rise to major sources of pollution that are degrading the marine environment as we have discussed. The direct and indirect by-products of fossil fuels used by consumers, industry and agriculture have found their way into our lakes, streams, rivers and oceans with deadly consequences.

Secondly, global warming, however fast it happens, will produce changes to our waters. For some these changes will be deadly. Higher tides from glacial melting and greater water temperature will result. In some lower areas of the world, like Bangladesh, for example, a rise in average tidal height of 1.5 feet means that the homes and lives of some six million people are put in jeopardy. Elongated, more intense hurricanes threaten a narrowing of "weather windows" for crossing oceans. Reduction of anchorages and shifts in current patterns that mariners have relied on for centuries are all part of other changes we can expect. While many of us may not live to see these happen, I hope all mariners are also concerned about the boating lives of our children, and future generations.

Boating and Global Warming

The current, unprecedented rise in the Earth's temperature, science tells us, is the result of more than a century of industrialization and humans burning fossil fuel for energy, releasing greenhouse gases (GHGs) as a result. These GHGs trap heat and warm the Earth. In truth it is nearly impossible to operate a boat today without contributing to these gases that cause global warming. Even the sailboat owner often has an outboard motor hanging off the transom or off the dinghy. And if that sailboat is fiberglass — well, fiberglass reinforced plastic (FRP), the most popular boat building material today, is made by combining fiberglass with a variety of polymers that are by-products of refining petroleum.

What's the answer? Should anyone who wants to boat be required to build a wooden kayak and use wooden paddles? I can already hear the cry of a vocal but impassioned extreme, Yes. But, then, since boats contribute a relatively small amount of GHGs to the environment when compared to cars, maybe we should be free to go about our love of boating with little or no concern about the effects of boating on the environment. Ahhh, I can also hear the cry of another vocal but impassioned extreme, Yes.

I believe the answer lies somewhere in the vast middle between these two impassioned extremes, and that is what this book is about.

When it comes to boating and environmental issues such as global warming, boaters themselves should lead the search for solutions that strike the proper balance of protecting the environment while promoting a lifestyle that we love. Call it sustainable boating, if you like, instead of boating green. And if the passion for boating is not enough motivation, there is always the profit of this pastime for some. Recreational boating is one of the fastest growing industries, generating sales of $40 billion a year in the United States alone. Certainly, it makes prudent financial sense to protect the environment that allows for this industry to flourish.

Boaters and Solutions to Global Warming

While it is important to "keep a weather eye" to global warming, it is also important not to be immobilized by a sense of hopelessness or resignation.

Boaters actually have a lot to offer when it comes to solutions. Boats, even more so than most homes, are independent microcosms of modern cities. They burn fossil fuel. They generate power. They create wastes. They produce pollutants. All are major human activities that are bringing about global warming. But that means how we boaters manage these activities is a model in miniature for how they can be handled on a larger scale.

One of the biggest arguments for not doing more about the causes of global warming is that solutions cost too much and, therefore, risk bringing about the ruin of industries and economies. But if the solutions we mariners can implement on our floating "micro cities" are any measures, just the opposite is true. Boating green is actually less costly. Maintenance and operation costs are reduced. Vessel safety is increased. Crew health is enhanced. And the environment reaps the benefits.

The bottom line with global warming is that we humans will need to change the way we go about many activities. Change can be a scary thing, particularly when others are exhorting you to change with strident or fear-based rhetoric. Sometimes the need to change is often best communicated by "doing" rather than "saying." As boaters, we actually make a loud statement about how to protect the environment and reduce the causes of global warming as we implement prudent, sensible approaches to maintaining and operating our boats. And, guess what? We're also enjoying our avocation in the process.

Steps You Can Take

- LEARN more about global warming and the degradation of the marine environment.
- IDENTIFY where and how you want to take actions that will make a difference.
- DECIDE when and where you will start.
- ACT on your knowledge and decisions.

Internet Search Terms

"global warming"; "myths about global warming"; "global warming" "marine environment"

Joint science academies' statement: Global response to climate change

Climate change is real

There will always be uncertainty in understanding a system as complex as the world's climate. However there is now strong evidence that significant global warming is occurring[1]. The evidence comes from direct measurements of rising surface air temperatures and subsurface ocean temperatures and from phenomena such as increases in average global sea levels, retreating glaciers, and changes to many physical and biological systems. It is likely that most of the warming in recent decades can be attributed to human activities (IPCC 2001)[2]. This warming has already led to changes in the Earth's climate.

The existence of greenhouse gases in the atmosphere is vital to life on Earth — in their absence average temperatures would be about 30 centigrade degrees lower than they are today. But human activities are now causing atmospheric concentrations of greenhouse gases — including carbon dioxide, methane, tropospheric ozone, and nitrous oxide — to rise well above pre-industrial levels. Carbon dioxide levels have increased from 280 ppm in 1750 to over 375 ppm today — higher than any previous levels that can be reliably measured (i.e. in the last 420,000 years). Increasing greenhouse gases are causing temperatures to rise; the Earth's surface warmed by approximately 0.6 centigrade degrees over the twentieth century. The Intergovernmental Panel on Climate Change (IPCC) projected that the average global surface temperatures will continue to increase to between 1.4 centigrade degrees and 5.8 centigrade degrees above 1990 levels, by 2100.

Reduce the causes of climate change

The scientific understanding of climate change is now sufficiently clear to justify nations taking prompt action. It is vital that all nations identify cost-effective steps that they can take now, to contribute to substantial and long-term reduction in net global greenhouse gas emissions.

Action taken now to reduce significantly the build-up of greenhouse gases in the atmosphere will lessen the magnitude and rate of climate change. As the United Nations Framework Convention on Climate Change (UNFCCC) recognises, a lack of full scientific certainty about some aspects of climate change is not a reason for delaying an immediate response that will, at a reasonable cost, prevent dangerous anthropogenic interference with the climate system.

As nations and economies develop over the next 25 years, world primary energy demand is estimated to increase by almost 60%. Fossil fuels, which are responsible for the majority of carbon dioxide emissions produced by human activities, provide valuable resources for many nations and are projected to provide 85% of this demand (IEA 2004)[3]. Minimizing the amount of this carbon dioxide reaching the atmosphere presents a huge challenge. There are many potentially cost-effective technological options that could contribute to stabilizing greenhouse gas concentrations. These are at various stages of research and development. However barriers to their broad deployment still need to be overcome.

Carbon dioxide can remain in the atmosphere for many decades. Even with possible lowered emission rates we will be experiencing the impacts of climate change throughout the 21st century and beyond. Failure to implement significant reductions in net greenhouse gas emissions now, will make the job much harder in the future.

Prepare for the consequences of climate change

Major parts of the climate system respond slowly to changes in greenhouse gas concentrations. Even if greenhouse gas emissions were stabilized instantly at today's levels, the climate would still continue to change as it adapts to the increased emission of recent decades. Further changes in climate are therefore unavoidable. Nations must prepare for them.

The projected changes in climate will have both beneficial and adverse effects at the regional level, for example on water resources, agriculture, natural ecosystems and human health. The larger and faster the changes in climate, the more likely it is that adverse effects will dominate. Increasing temperatures are likely to increase the frequency and severity of weather events such as heat waves and heavy rainfall. Increasing temperatures could lead to large-scale effects such as melting of large ice sheets (with major impacts on low-lying regions throughout the world). The IPCC estimates that the combined effects of ice melting and sea water expansion from ocean warming are projected to cause the global mean sea-level to rise by between 0.1 and 0.9 meters between 1990 and 2100. In Bangladesh alone, a 0.5 meter sea-level rise would place about 6 million people at risk from flooding.

Developing nations that lack the infrastructure or resources to respond to the impacts of climate change will be particularly affected. It is clear that many of the world's poorest people are likely to suffer the most from climate change. Long-term global efforts to create a more healthy, prosperous and sustainable world may be severely hindered by changes in the climate.

The task of devising and implementing strategies to adapt to the consequences of climate change will require worldwide collaborative inputs from a wide range of experts, including physical and natural scientists, engineers, social scientists, medical scientists, those in the humanities, business leaders and economists.

Conclusion

We urge all nations, in line with the UNFCCC principles[4], to take prompt action to reduce the causes of climate change, adapt to its impacts and ensure that the issue is included in all relevant national and international strategies. As national science academies, we commit to working with governments to help develop and implement the national and international response to the challenge of climate change.

G8 nations have been responsible for much of the past greenhouse gas emissions. As parties to the UNFCCC, G8 nations are committed to showing leadership in addressing climate change and assisting developing nations to meet the challenges of adaptation and mitigation.

We call on world leaders, including those meeting at the Gleneagles G8 Summit in July 2005, to:

- Acknowledge that the threat of climate change is clear and increasing.
- Launch an international study[5] to explore scientifically informed targets for atmospheric greenhouse gas concentrations, and their associated emissions scenarios, that will enable nations to avoid impacts deemed unacceptable.
- Identify cost-effective steps that can be taken now to contribute to substantial and long-term reduction in net global greenhouse gas emissions. Recognise that delayed action will increase the risk of adverse environmental effects and will likely incur a greater cost.
- Work with developing nations to build a scientific and technological capacity best suited to their circumstances, enabling them to develop innovative solutions to mitigate and adapt to the adverse effects of climate change, while explicitly recognizing their legitimate development rights.
- Show leadership in developing and deploying clean energy technologies and approaches to energy efficiency, and share this knowledge with all other nations.
- Mobilize the science and technology community to enhance research and development efforts, which can better inform climate change decisions.

Notes and references

1 This statement concentrates on climate change associated with global warming. We use the UNFCCC definition of climate change, which is 'a change of climate which is attributed directly or

indirectly to human activity that alters the composition of the global atmosphere and which is in addition to natural climate variability observed over comparable time periods.'

2   IPCC (2001). Third Assessment Report. We recognize the international scientific consensus of the Intergovernmental Panel on Climate Change (IPCC).

3   IEA (2004). World Energy Outlook 4. Although long-term projections of future world energy demand and supply are highly uncertain, the World Energy Outlook produced by the International Energy Agency (IEA) is a useful source of information about possible future energy scenarios.

4   With special emphasis on the first principle of the UNFCCC, which states: 'The Parties should protect the climate system for the benefit of present and future generations of humankind, on the basis of equity and in accordance with their common but differentiated responsibilities and respective capabilities. Accordingly, the developed country Parties should take the lead in combating climate change and the adverse effects thereof.'

5   Recognizing and building on the IPCC's ongoing work on emission scenarios.

Academia Brasiliera de Ciências
Brazil

Royal Society of Canada,
Canada

Chinese Academy of Sciences,
China

Academié des Sciences,
France

Deutsche Akademie der Naturforscher
Leopoldina, Germany

Indian National Science Academy,
India

Accademia dei Lincei,
Italy

Science Council of Japan,
Japan

Russian Academy of Sciences,
Russia

Royal Society,
United Kingdom

National Academy of Sciences,
United States of America

CHAPTER 6

One Boater Can Make a Difference

The actions of individuals and the commons.

E conomist Garrett Hardin tells the following story to illustrate a point[1]:

> Imagine a large pasture that is open to all. Each herdsman
> will try to keep as many cattle as possible grazing on this
> commons. Such an arrangement may work well for centuries
> because tribal wars, poaching and disease keep the numbers
> of both man and beast well below the carrying capacity of
> the land. One day, the long-desired goal of social stability
> becomes a reality. Wars are not as prevalent. Technology has
> created sophisticated methods of genetic identification that
> make poaching difficult. Advances in medicine have helped
> to conquer disease. Still each herdsman asks himself, "What's
> the benefit *to me* of adding just one more animal to my
> herd?" The conclusion the herdsman reaches is that one more
> animal will result in increased profits to him when the animal
> is sold and minimal overgrazing of the land since all share
> this large common pasture. So he adds an animal to his herd.
> And another …. But each and every rational herdsman shar-
> ing the commons reaches this same conclusion. And therein
> lies the tragedy: each man is locked into a way of thinking
> that has him increasing his herd without limit — in a world
> that is limited. Ultimately, the commons will be overgrazed

and no herdsmen will be able to raise his cattle. Pursuing one's own best interest in a society that believes in the freedom of the commons brings ruin to all.

Garrett called this conundrum the "Tragedy of the Commons." He used this story to illustrate the challenges of unlimited increased population growth in a world that has limited resources. But it has also been applied to a host of other problems like over-fishing, habitat degradation of sensitive species, petroleum utilization and the decline of the health of the marine environment.

Consider that our waterways (oceans, rivers, lakes) are our commons and we boaters are among the many users of that commons. And now let's look at the question of waste disposal in our commons. Each user asks himself, What is the benefit *to me* of dumping my waste into this commons? On one hand, the benefit is great because our waterways appear to provide a ready cost-free solution for human waste. The drawbacks seem minimal because the commons (oceans, rivers, lakes) appear huge. But each and every user of our common waterways reaches the same conclusion and dumps more and more waste. Certainly, for years humans have been using the oceans, rivers and lakes for waste disposal. Like the commons used for centuries by the herdsmen, this can work up to a point. But when the carrying capacity of the waterways reaches its limit, tragedy sets in and the waterways decline to a point where they are of use to no one. Our waterways are fast reaching that point. And though we boaters contribute just a small amount to the problem of waste pollution in our waters, we can be among those who turn this potential tragedy of the commons into a triumph of the commons by our willingness to take actions that reverse the steady decline of the marine environment. Each boater can make a difference.

The Triumph of the Commons

Legendary folksinger Pete Seeger lives along the Hudson River. In 1966 it was among the most polluted rivers in the country. That year Seeger set out to "build a boat to save the river." He constructed a 106-foot wooden schooner, the S/V *Clearwater*, and sailed her up and down the Hudson as a platform for educating the public and elected representatives about the problems of degradation to our waterways, and the need to pass national legislation to reverse the decline of our nation's waterways.[2]

In 1970 S/V *Clearwater* sailed to Washington, DC with Pete and fellow musician Don McLean to highlight the plight of the Hudson and the need to protect our waterways. Seeger led the Clearwater organization's constituents in collecting petitions, writing elected officials and lobbying for the passage of a law known as the Clean Water Act. It offered a long-term solution to the health of the nation's waters beyond simply punitive fines for polluters.

Seeger articulated in words and music his vision of a fully restored Hudson. He sang songs, spoke to thousands and galvanized mass national support for the Clean Water Act, signed into law by President Richard Nixon in 1972. Propelled by Seeger's vision, Clearwater members have initiated or joined virtually every significant battle to protect and restore the Hudson River, its estuary, tributaries and wetlands. To date that Clean Water Act has been one of the most effective pieces of environmental legislation helping in the cleanup of rivers, lakes and bays around the country. Although the struggle for a cleaner Hudson River still continues, fish habitat has returned in many portions, and it is demonstrably cleaner than it was before Pete Seeger began his efforts.

Since adoption of the Act, Seeger's fight to save the Hudson has grown into an innovative template for environmental education and protection. More than 400,000 school children and tens of thousands of adults have sailed aboard the *Clearwater* locally, and dozens of national and international programs have been modeled after the ship-based environmental education programs pioneered by Clearwater.

All boaters owe Seeger and his Clearwater organization a debt of gratitude not only because our waters are cleaner, but also because he showed us that one boater can make a difference.

Resources
See chapter 49 for a complete list of organizations working for the health of our waterways.

CHapTeR 7

Make Sure Your Vessel Complies with Coast Guard Regulations

Safety and pollution regulations for Canadian and American boaters.

A merican and Canadian boaters are required to meet minimum safety and pollution standards set forth by the coast guards of their respective countries. These regulations are designed to protect the health and safety of boaters and to protect the marine environment. All boaters are required to stop, when asked by a coast guard patrol, and to allow their vessel to be boarded. Coast guard boarding parties will check that these minimum standards are met.

US Coast Guard Safety Regulations

Minimum US Coast Guard safety and pollution regulations for recreational boats cover the use of personal flotation devices (PFDs), visual distress signals, fire extinguishers, sound-producing devices and navigational lights. For the sake of completeness, all of the minimum Coast Guard safety equipment regulations are presented in a table on page 34. Although some are more directly related to environmental protection, others are more directly related to vessel operator and crew health and safety.

Canadian Coast Guard Safety Regulations

Canadian Coast Guard safety regulations, also aimed at protection of boaters and the environment, differ slightly from their American counterparts.

Required USCG Safety Equipment for Recreational Vessels
Table 7.1

REQUIRED EQUIPMENT	BOAT LENGTH			
Consult USCG Regulations for details	Personal Watercraft	Less than 16 feet	16 to 26 feet	26 to 65 feet
PFD - Type I, II, III, or IV wearable for each person	☐	☐	☐	☐
PFD - throwable (seat cushion/ring buoy)		☐	☐	☐
Fire Extinguishers	☐	☐	☐	☐
Cut-off Safety Device	☐	Recommended		
Flame Arrestor (gasoline inboard)		☐	☐	☐
Ventilation System		☐	☐	☐
Muffler	☐	☐	☐	☐
Sound Producing Device	☐	☐	☐	☐
Visual Distress (Day) - coastal waters	Recommended		☐	☐
Visual Distress (Night) - coastal waters		☐	☐	☐
Marine Sanitation Device for toilet (see section of this book on MSDs)		☐	☐	☐
Navigation Lights		☐	☐	☐

Canadian Coast Guard Safety Regulations.
Table 7.2

REQUIRED EQUIPMENT	BOAT LENGTH				
Consult Canadian Coast Guard regulations for details	< 6 m (motorized)	< 6 m (non-motorized)	6 -8 m	8–12 m	12-20 m
PFD that fits each person	☐	☐	☐	☐	☐
Buoyant heaving line 15m	☐	☐	☐	☐	☐
Manual propelling device OR an anchor 15m	☐	☐	☐		

Canadian Coast Guard Safety Regulations cont.

REQUIRED EQUIPMENT	BOAT LENGTH				
				30 m	50 m
Anchor (chain, rope, cable)				30 m	50 m
Bailer OR manual water pump with hose	☐	☐	☐	☐	☐
1 fire extinguisher Class 5BC	if equipped w/inboard engine, fixed fuel tank OR fuel burning appliance	if equipped with fuel burning appliance	2 if power-driven AND equipped with fuel burning appliance		
1 fire extinguisher Class 10BC				2 if power-driven AND equipped with fuel burning appliance	• All spaces with fuel burning or refrigerating appliance • Entrance to staterooms • Entrance to the engine room
Watertight flashlight	✓, or 3 flares of type A, B or C		☐	☐	☐
Reboarding device			☐	☐	☐
Flares	3 flares of type A, B or C OR watertight flashlight		6 flares of type A, B, or C if vessel can be > 1mile offshore	12 Canadian-approved flares of Type A, B, C or D, no more than six (6) of.which are of Type D	
Fire Axe					☐
10L buckets (2)					☐
Sound signaling equipment	☐	☐	☐	☐	☐
Navigation lights	☐	☐	☐	☐	☐
Radar Reflector	Required for vessels constructed primarily of non-metallic materials unless they are not essential to the safety of the vessel, or the small size of the vessel or its operation away from radar navigation makes compliance impractical.				

US Pollution Regulations

Regulations protecting the marine environment from pollution have been in place for more than a century. The Refuse Act of 1899 prohibited throwing, discharging or depositing any refuse matter of any kind (including trash, garbage, oil and other liquid pollutants) into the waters of the United States. The MARPOL (Marine Pollution) Convention is the main international convention covering prevention of pollution of the marine environment by ships from operational or accidental causes. It is a combination of two treaties adopted by most countries in 1973 and 1978 respectively and updated by amendments through the years.

The US Federal Water Pollution Control Acts and amendments of 1972 and 1977 (collectively known as the Clean Water Act) prohibit the discharge of oil or hazardous substances that may be harmful into US navigable waters. Vessels longer than 26 feet must display a placard at least five-by-eight inches, made of durable material, fixed in a conspicuous place in the machinery spaces or at the bilge pump control station, stating the following:

> Regulations issued under the Federal Water Pollution Control Act require all vessels with propulsion machinery to have a capacity to retain oily mixtures on board. A fixed or portable means to discharge oily waste to a reception facility is required. A bucket or bailer is suitable as a portable means of discharging oily waste on recreational vessels. No person may intentionally drain oil or oily waste from any source into the bilge of any vessel.

You must immediately notify the US Coast Guard if your vessel discharges oil or hazardous substances in the water. Call toll-free 1-800-

Discharge of Oil Prohibited

The Federal Water Pollution Control Act prohibits the discharge of oil or oily waste upon or into any navigable waters of the US. The prohibition includes any discharge which causes a film or discoloration of the surface of the water or causes a sludge or emulsion beneath the surface of the water. Violators are subjected to substantial civil and/or criminal sanctions including fines and imprisonment.

424-8802 (in Washington, DC (202) 267-2675). Report the following information:

1. location   4. color
2. source   5. substances
3. size   6. time observed

From a regulatory standpoint, any spill (even olive oil) is reportable. In order for a penalty to be assessed, the amount spilled has to be a "harmful quantity." "Harmful," according to the regulations, means any amount that violates applicable water quality standards; or causes a FILM, SHEEN, SLUDGE, EMULSION or DISCOLORATION upon a navigable waterway of the United States. See chapter 11 for more on the steps to take in the event of an oil spill.

Regulations Controlling Disposal of Garbage
United States

US Coast Guard regulations prohibit dumping of plastic refuse and garbage mixed with plastic into any waters. These restrictions apply to all US vessels wherever they operate (except waters under the exclusive jurisdiction of a State) and any foreign vessels operating in US waters out to and including the Exclusive Economic Zone (200 miles).

The Act to Prevent Pollution from Ships (MARPOL ANNEX V) places limitations on the discharge of garbage from vessels. It is illegal to dump plastic trash anywhere in the ocean or navigable waters of the

Garbage disposal regulations.

GARBAGE TYPE	PROHIBITED
Plastics — includes synthetic ropes, fishing nets and plastic bags	All areas
Floating dunnage, lining and packing materials	Inside 25 miles from nearest land
Food waste, paper, rags, glass, metal, bottles, crockery and similar refuse	Inside 12 miles from nearest land
Plastic, dunnage, lining and packing materials that float and any garbage except dishwater/ graywater/fresh fish parts.	Inside 3 miles from nearest land

Table 7.3

United States. It is also illegal to discharge garbage in the navigable waters of the United States, including inland waters, as well as anywhere in the Great Lakes. The discharge of other types of garbage is permitted outside of specific distances offshore, as determined by the nature of that garbage.

United States vessels of 26 feet or longer must display in a prominent location a durable SOS (Save Our Seas) placard at least four-by-nine inches notifying the crew and passengers of the discharge restrictions.

Canada

Canada is a signatory to the MARPOL Convention, and thus the garbage pollution restrictions shown in Table 7.2 apply to Canadian boaters as well. Transport Canada maintains a searchable database of marine waste disposal sites at www.tc.gc.ca/MarineSafety/Ships-and-operations-standards/mwrf/default_e.asp

Did You Know?

- Dunnage, material used to block and brace cargo, is considered a cargo-associated waste.
- Vessels over 40 feet are required to carry a Waste Management Plan. The Plan must be in writing and describe procedures for collecting, processing, storing and properly disposing of garbage in a way that will not violate the requirement. It must also designate the person who is in charge of carrying out the plan.

Resources

Code of Federal Regulations (CFR) Title 46 Shipping, Volume 1, Chapter 1, especially Part 25: http://www.access.gpo.gov/cgi-bin/cfrassemble.cgi?title=200446. A detailed description of all applicable United States Coast Guard regulations and requirements.

Consolidated Regulations of Canada (CRC), Volume XVII, c. 1987: www.tc.gc.ca/acts-regulations/GENERAL/C/CSA/regulations/070/ csa076/csa76.html. A detailed description of all applicable Canadian Coast Guard regulations and requirements.

Internet Search Terms

MARPOL; USCG pollution regulations; Canada Coast Guard pollution regulations; USCG boating safety; Canada boating safety

CHAPTER 8

Maintain Situational Awareness

Situational Awareness promotes safety
and environmental protection.

"Situational Awareness" is a term most commonly associated with the military, especially aviation, where it's defined as one's awareness of the surroundings, circumstances and tactical situation. Fighter pilots are trained that Situational Awareness (SA for short) is crucial to their effectiveness and safety. Studies have shown that a major factor separating top guns from good pilots is the degree to which they are capable of exercising and maintaining Situational Awareness. Anyone who's driven a car is familiar with SA and its implications, particularly since the advent of cellphones. If you decide to make a cellphone call while you're driving, you probably know that your effectiveness as a safe driver diminishes significantly. Operating a cellphone while driving a car reduces SA. That's why many jurisdictions have banned the use of hand-held cellphones while driving.

Actually Situational Awareness is more complex than any of the above scenarios. While we may talk about having or not having SA, it's best to think of it as a skill rather than a commodity. Like playing a violin or docking a boat in close quarters, SA is a skill that can be learned, practiced and perfected.

What does SA have to do with protecting the marine environment? Consider the following scenario. Two boaters pull up to the fuel dock in similar late-model 42-foot vessels, sleek, white and gleaming in the sun. One boater has his music blaring. His guests are aboard moving to the groove of the beat. He spins off the deck fill cap, takes the fuel nozzle from the attendant and thrusts it into the fuel port, snapping his fingers and wriggling his body while he fills his tank. Meanwhile the other boater turns off his music and asks everyone to step off. He attaches a "catch cup" underneath his fuel overflow port. Finally, he takes the fuel nozzle from the attendant and pokes it through a hole in an absorbent pad before inserting it into the filling port.

Which of these two boaters do you think is more likely to have a fuel spill or other accident? If an accident does occur, which of these two boaters is more likely to respond in a timely, appropriate manner that reduces harm to others and to the environment? Which of these two boaters displays greater Situational Awareness?

Whether it's filling up at the fuel dock, performing an oil change or touching up your brightwork, many of the routine activities that boaters perform have the potential to cause physical and environmental harm. Beyond simply "knowing what you're doing," maintaining Situational Awareness reduces the likelihood of accidents occurring and enables us to respond more quickly and appropriately when they do.

The GAR Model of SA

The Coast Guard trains its personnel in a simple, intuitive procedure for Situational Awareness, called *GAR*, short for *Green-Amber-Red*. When anyone aboard a vessel encounters a situation they believe may impact the safety of the crew or the environment, they categorize it as either "Green," meaning continue despite the situation, or "Amber" meaning proceed while paying caution to the situation and addressing it later, or "Red" meaning stop to address the situation before continuing. All conditions are immediately brought to the attention of the vessel captain or watchstander with the observer's classification of the event. The captain or watchstander, of course, may classify the event differently.

In practice, GAR might work like this. Let's say you're in command of a

Stop: Address situation before proceeding.

Caution: Proceed with heightened awareness.

Continue: Address situation at later point.

Fig. 8.1: *GAR Model of Situational Awareness*

vessel and you've been running straight for almost eight hours. A family member notices through a portal into the engine room that a plastic container sitting on top of the engine has filled up with a greenish liquid when it is normally empty. They report the situation to you as Amber. You thank them for maintaining a high degree of Situational Awareness, ask them to take the helm for a moment and go to check on the situation yourself. After donning sound-protective ear guards you step into the engine room and realize that heated coolant has overflowed into the expansion container, just as it should. Back at the helm, you report to the family member your findings and that you're reclassifying the situation as Green, but that you are also going to check coolant levels more closely once you arrive at your next port of call.

In this scenario, the actions of the captain and crew have enhanced the safety of everyone aboard, lessened the potential for severe engine damage and reduced the likelihood of releasing coolant laden with antifreeze into the bilge and eventually into the water. Similar situations might arise when someone aboard notices and reports engine oil leaks, hydraulic leaks, foul odors from a head or strange sounds. Situational Awareness is the responsibility of every crew member aboard a vessel, not just the captain or watch-stander. Asking crew members to classify and report anything they observe that seems out of the ordinary should be a standard part of every vessel safety briefing.

Resource
Clyde W. Ford. "Situational Awareness and Boating." *Passagemaker Magazine,* Nov/Dec 2006.

Internet Search Term
"Situational Awareness"

CHAPTER 9

A Personal Vision of Protecting
Our Waters

Create your personal vision statement for
protecting our waters.

C reating a personal vision statement of what protecting the marine
environment means is an empowering tool that will support any
other steps you take. This statement can express your hopes and desires
about protecting the marine environment; it can also express your concerns and fears. A personal vision can take many forms — an affirmation,
a prayer, a poem, a song, a painting, a ritual or any other form of cre-
ative expression. It need not be long, but it should come from your
deepest feelings and convictions about the importance of protecting
the marine environment. Your personal vision is something you can
come back to again and again.

A Sample Personal Vision of Protecting the Marine Environment

I have derived so much enjoyment from my time spent on the water
boating, fishing, observing wildlife, visiting remote areas. I would like
these same opportunities to be available to my children and to coming
generations. I realize the marine environment is fragile and that its
health is declining for many reasons. To the extent possible, I will
maintain and operate my boat in such a way that I minimize further
degradation to the marine environment. Through my example, I hope
to inspire other boaters to do the same.

Ideas for a Personal Vision Statement

- List three ways in which you have derived pleasure or enjoyment from boating and being on the water.
- List three steps you will take to minimize further deterioration of the marine environment.
- Draw a picture that reflects your vision of protecting the marine environment (an especially good activity for children).
- List some of the benefits you hope to obtain from operating and maintaining your boat in a way that protects the marine environment: decreased maintenance costs, better performance, enhanced safety, more enjoyable time on the water.

Steps You Can Take

- Create you personal vision statement.
- Keep it somewhere on your boat so that you can refer to it periodically.
- Change you personal vision statement as your awareness and actions to protect the marine environment evolve.

The Power of Personal Vision

If a personal vision statement seems a bit far-fetched or too new-age, consider that in the 1960s it was folksinger and boater Pete Seeger's personal vision statement, made public through his letters, songs and the construction of a 106-foot schooner, the S/V *Clearwater*, that led directly to the passage of the Clean Water Act, a milestone in protecting our waters that boaters and our society are enjoying the benefits from today. Personal vision statements can inspire boaters and everyone interested in saving our waters to act to make a difference.

OPERATING YOUR VESSEL

MARY JANE JESSEN

CHAPTER 10

Fill 'er Up!

Every fuel stop is an opportunity to
practice marine stewardship.

M ore spills occur while fueling a boat than during any other activity. Most boaters know the feeling of pulling up to fuel dock, being handed the nozzle of a fuel line and seeing a small geyser erupt from the on-deck fuel fill or drip out the vent.

For safety reasons, boat fuel tanks are not pressurized like car fuel tanks. Nozzles do not automatically stop, and fuel often runs through the pump much faster at the fuel dock than at the gas station. The two most prevalent places for a fuel spill to occur are from the tank vent and the fuel-fill port. But there are steps you can take to reduce the likelihood of a fuel spill occurring while you're filling up your tanks. Many of the following steps come from the Boat US "Stop the Drop" campaign.[1]

Steps You Can Take

Before fueling:

- Check your fuel vent lines regularly for blockages, kinks or low spots. A blocked vent line is a frequent cause of the small fuel geysers that erupt through your filling port.
- Install a fuel/air separator in your vent line. This is a device which allows air, but not fuel, to escape from the vent.
- Install a vented deck fill that recycles vented fuel back into the tank preventing an overflow.

- Put out all smoking materials and secure your boat to the dock.
- Know how much fuel your boat holds and how much you need.
- Turn off engine(s), electronics; extinguish all open flames.
- Send passengers ashore and close hatches, ports and doors.
- Remove portable tank(s) from boat and fill on the dock.

During fueling:

- Assure that you have selected the type of fuel you need.
- Be certain that fuel is going into the proper fill entry.
- Use an absorbent pad or donut around deck fill to catch spills. You can buy a donut or a bib made especially for this purpose or simply make your own on the spot. Double over an oil-absorbent pad and make a hole in it just wide enough to insert the fuel nozzle. After filling use the pad to clean up any fuel drips.
- Use a donut or collar if you're filling up your outboard.
- Don't fill up your dinghy's outboard directly over the water. If it's attached to boat, swing it around so the fuel cap is inside the dinghy. Place an oil-absorbent pad on the floor of the dinghy underneath the fill cap while you're fueling. If you're filling your dinghy while you're on land, place oil-absorbent pads on the ground under the fill cap.
- Catch spills from the fuel vent with inexpensive collection containers that attach via suction to the hull of your boat beneath the vent.
- Maintain contact between nozzle and deck fill to prevent sparking.
- Hold the nozzle when refueling — don't use a hands-free clip.
- Fuel slowly and listen for a change in tone as the tank gets full. If you're unsure of how full you are, stop fueling completely, then start again. This is also a good strategy if you suddenly realize your vent line may be clogged.
- Don't rely on the automatic shut-off device — marina fuel pumps fuel at a faster rate than land-based pumps — they often don't shut off in time.
- Resist topping off — as the temperature rises, fuel expands. Fill tanks to 90% capacity to leave room for expansion.
- Avoid turning on the switch for the fuel gauge (or any other switch) while refueling. Turning on any electronics while fueling is dangerous and can increase the risk of sparking.

- Do not use a cellphone (or allow your passengers to use one) during fueling. Explosions have taken place because of cellphone use while fueling a car.

After fueling:

- Wipe up all spills and drips on deck from the overboard fuel vent. Dispose of pads properly.
- Do not use detergents to disperse a sheen or spill on the water — it's illegal.
- Open ports, hatches and doors to ventilate.
- Before starting engine, operate blower for 3-5 minutes.
- Sniff bilges and engine compartment for fumes.

In general:

- Limit exposure to fumes and avoid skin contact.
- Always watch and listen for cues that your tank is nearing capacity and stop before any fuel can escape.
- Wipe up spills immediately. Spilled fuel can ruin gelcoat, paint, striping, trim and upholstery.
- Gasoline vapors are heavier than air and can spread rapidly into enclosed spaces. Gasoline vapors can burn or explode if sparked. Proper fueling procedures are extremely important in preventing onboard fires.

Internet Search Terms
"fuel spills"; "fuel dock"; "fuel/air separator"; "fueling tips" boaters

CHaPTeR 11

Oil Spill Reporting and Prevention

Learn the response process and how to
create a spill kit.

Accidents happen even to the most environmentally conscious, well-prepared boaters. The actions you take when a spill happens can make a big difference in the consequences to the environment and to you. Act to prevent spills but be prepared for when they happen. Know your responsibilities. Follow through with quick decisive actions.

Responding to an Oil Spill

If you have an accidental oil spill, or you are the first person on the scene of an oil spill, here are some guidelines you should follow:

- In still or slow-moving water, if you can safely reach the spill, place oil-absorbent materials that float on the water surface. Lightly sweep an oil-absorbent pad over the water surface to soak up as much oil as possible. Use bilge socks to form an oil boom that prevents the oil from spreading. Don't leave these items to float away, creating hazardous litter.
- If your engine or fuel system has an oil leak, stop at the nearest mooring place for repairs.
- If your bilge is pumping out oil, and there is no danger of your vessel taking on additional water, stop the bilge pump until you can find the source of the oil. Stop the oil leak, if possible. Clean oil from the bilge before turning the pump on.

- Don't mix detergent with the oil. This will make the pollution worse by emulsifying the oil and allowing it to spread more easily in the marine environment.
- After mitigating the spill as much as possible, follow the reporting rules above and call the NRC or other applicable agencies.

Notify the US National Response Center

Section 311(b)(3) of the Clean Water Act prohibits the discharge of oil into or upon navigable waters of the United States or adjoining shorelines in harmful quantities. As soon as the captain, mariner or person in charge of a vessel has knowledge of such a discharge, he or she must notify the National Response Center, which then notifies the US Coast Guard and agencies of the affected State. Additional statutory provisions and regulations adopted by the US EPA and the US Coast Guard define the important terms of this notification requirement:

1. *Discharge* means any spilling, leaking, pumping, pouring, emitting, emptying or dumping, but excluding such discharges in compliance with a permit. See 33 U.S.C. § 1321(a)(2).
2. *Oil.* Any kind of oil, in any form, including petroleum, fuel oil, sludge, oil refuse and oils mixed with wastes. US EPA also interprets the term to include crude oil and petroleum-refined products. Biodiesel and even vegetable oil spills could qualify as reportable incidents. See 33 U.S.C. § 1321(a)(1).
3. *Navigable waters of the United States* is defined by judicial decision and EPA regulations to reach the outer boundaries of interstate commerce. Thus, it includes not only interstate waters, but waters that are located solely within a single state, such as lakes, rivers and streams that are adjacent to and might be used in connection with interstate commerce.
4. *Harmful quantities* means any quantity of oil discharge that: (a) violates a water quality standard; (b) causes sludge or emulsion to be deposited beneath the surface of the water; or (c) *causes a film or sheen upon, or discoloration of, the surface of the water* (author's italics). (Referred to as the "sheen test.") See 40 C.F.R. 110.3.
5. *Exemptions* from the reporting requirements are granted for properly functioning vessel engines; research and development

releases; NPDES-permitted releases (National Pollution Discharge Elimination System); and certain discharges beyond the territorial seas permitted by MARPOL (International Convention for the Prevention of Pollution from Ships).

In the US vessel operators, or those witnessing a reportable spill, are required to call the National Response Center (NRC) at (800) 424-8804. On the west coast, POSPET, the Pacific Oil Spills Prevention Education Team, has set-up (800) OILS-911 as a reporting number where calls will be directed to appropriate authorities in either the US or British Columbia (otherwise the reporting number in BC is (800) 889-8852). Your report will eventually wind up with the US or Canadian Coast Guard and applicable agencies in your state or province through a process that often takes just minutes. The NRC is staffed 24 hours a day by US Coast Guard personnel who will ask you to provide as much information about the incident as possible, including:

1. Your name, location, organization and telephone number
2. Name and address of the party responsible for the incident
3. Date and time of the incident
4. Location of the incident
5. Source and cause of the release or spill
6. Types of material(s) released or spilled
7. Quantity of materials released or spilled
8. Medium (e.g., land, water) affected by release or spill
9. Danger or threat posed by the release or spill
10. Number and types of injuries or fatalities (if any)
11. Weather conditions at the incident location
12. Name of the carrier or vessel, the railcar/truck number or other identifying information
13. Whether an evacuation has occurred
14. Other agencies notified or about to be notified
15. Any other information that may help emergency personnel respond to the incident

If you are unable to call in to the NRC, you can use emergency channel 16 to contact the nearest Coast Guard station to report the spill.

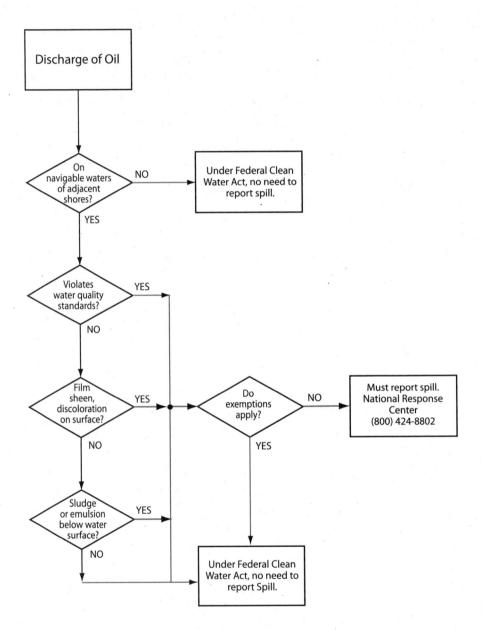

Fig. 11.1: *Flowchart for reporting oil spills. Note: An oil spill that is not reportable under the Federal Clean Water Act may still be reportable under State and local regulations. Check with your local Coast Guard station or State.*

Contact the Canadian Coast Guard

While boating in Canadian waters, you should report oil spills to the Canadian Coast Guard via VHF channel 16 or by phone: in the Yukon and BC, (800) 889-8852; in Quebec, (800) 363-4735; in the Maritimes, (800) 565-1582; in Newfoundland, (800) 563-2444; and in all other provinces, (800) 265-0237.

Flowchart for Reporting Spills

Confused about whether a spill that happened is reportable? Follow the flowchart in Figure 11.1.

Coast Guard Response

US Coast Guard personnel handle reports of spills on a case-by-case basis. Overall policies are in place, but some discretion is available to the officer assigned to your case. His or her ultimate decision will depend on many factors, including:

1. How soon you reported the spill. Did you wait a week, or did you report the spill immediately?
2. The actions you took immediately following the spill. See the sections below for mitigating actions that you can take in the event of a spill.
3. How much oil was spilled? Did you spill a few ounces or several thousand gallons?
4. What is the likely environmental damage caused by your spill?
5. How professionally did you interact with the regulatory agencies? There are cases of belligerent boaters being issued stiff fines for spilling two or three ounces of fuel oil at the dock. While overzealous enforcement may be at play, it behooves you to report all facts of the situation in a professional, courteous manner. Complaints about your treatment by Coast Guard personnel can be directed to the commandant of the Coast Guard district you reside in.

The US Coast Guard adjudicates the response to your report of the spill. If you are the party liable for the spill there are three options open to the Coast Guard:

1. *Issue a warning.* This is generally done for unintentional spills of less than 100 gallons where there is minimal environmental damage.
2. *Issue a ticket.* Ticket fees range from $50 to $500 for spills that the Coast Guard considers more negligent.
3. *Issue a civil fine.* For large, deliberate spills the civil fines can range up to $25,000.

Spill Prevention

With phone calls to make, paperwork to file, possible fines to face and the potential for environmental damage, wouldn't it be better to prevent spills in the first place? Many of the sections in this book include very specific steps that you can take to prevent oil spills from your boat. Here are some general steps:

- Keep the engine well-tuned and operating efficiently.
- Practice preventative engine maintenance. Inspect fuel lines, hoses, hydraulic lines, valves, oil seals, gaskets and connections for deterioration and leaks. Fix leaks and replace worn parts. When replacing hoses, new sections should be the right length to prevent damage and leaks. Properly secure lines and hoses to prevent chaffing, abrasion and damage.
- Choose Coast Guard-approved alcohol-resistant fuel lines. These are critical for gasoline engines that may operate on ethanol. See chapter 13 for more details on ethanol.
- Install drip pans under all equipment that might leak.
- Avoid using solvents or toxic chemicals to clean engine parts. Use mechanical means (such as hand-scraping caked oil) or less-toxic solvents (water-based). Do not let solvent run into the bilge.
- Transfer and remove fluids with care, using funnels, pumps and absorbents to eliminate drips and spills and to keep the bilge clean.
- Never use soaps or detergents to clean oil or fuel spills; it is illegal and increases the pollution problem by dispersing the oil into the water more easily.
- Install an onboard bilge filtration system that filters gas, oil or diesel from bilge water before the automatic pump discharges the water.
- Use oil-only absorbents in the bilge, securely fastened to prevent clogging the bilge pump or its sensor, to capture unexpected leaks. If you have a large quantity of oil in the bilge, use a bilge pump-out system.

- Never use the sewage pump-out for the bilge
- If the bilge and/or engine compartment still needs significant cleaning after bilge pump-out, use a steam-cleaning service.

Create an Oil Spill Kit for Your Vessel

You can purchase an oil spill kit from an industrial supply store or chandlery.[1] For a lot less money, you can make your own. A spill kit usually contains two or three types of equipment:

- Personal Protective Equipment (PPE), clothing and other protective gear for the person responding to the spill.
- Equipment used to clean up the spill.
- Equipment to stop the spill or leak.

A Small Spill Kit for Every Vessel

1. Several pairs of latex or nitrile gloves.
2. Oil absorbent such as pads, bilge socks or small oil booms.
3. Nitrile sheets, hose clamps, scissors to stop a leak that may be coming from a broken oil line.
4. A container to collect and store the clean-up material.
5. A whisk broom, a dust pan and a heavy-duty plastic bag to line your collection container. By keeping it clean, you may be able to reuse it.

All of this should easily fit inside a two- or five-gallon covered plastic pail, which should be labeled so anyone can clearly identify it as a spill kit. Place the cover on loosely to keep the contents dry and clean but allow the pail to be easily opened. Pack the contents in layers from bottom to top:

- Layer 1: Any clean-up equipment needed after working on the leak.
- Layer 2: Any equipment used to stop the leak.
- Layer 3: Absorbent materials; they will be deployed first.
- Layer 4: Protective gloves on top, since this is the first item that a responder will need.

Internet Search Terms

"oil spill"; "recreational boating"; "National Response Center"; "Coast Guard"; "oil spills"; "oil absorbent pads"; "bilge socks"; "oil spill kits"; "Federal Clean Water Act"

CHAPTER 12

Use Biodiesel

Biodiesel benefits you, your boat and the environment.

The use of vegetable oil for engine fuels may seem insignificant today. But such oils may become in the course of time as important as petroleum.

— Rudolph Diesel, inventor of the diesel engine, 1912

The fuel dock operator in Campbell River, British Columbia, laughed as he told of fishing with his father during World War II. "There was no fuel to purchase," he said, "so my dad would pour olive oil, kerosene or heating oil into the tank. 'As long as it would combust,' he said, 'the engine would run.'"

The fisherman was correct. Diesel engines operate by highly compressing air within each cylinder. This raises the temperature within the cylinder to temperatures between 1300° and 1650°F (700° - 900°C). *Any* combustible fuel injected into the cylinder then ignites to power the engine. In fact, in the 1890s, Rudolph Diesel first designed his engines to run on vegetable oil — peanut oil to be exact. He envisioned a future that relied on plant-based fuels as opposed to fossil-based fuels.

Biodiesel

Biodiesel is a non-toxic, biodegradable replacement for petroleum diesel that comes from organic material. While soybean oil is a popular source of biodiesel, it is not the only one. Vegetables, peanuts, palm trees, rapeseed, canola, used restaurant oils or even tallow (animal fat) are just some of the other possible sources. Biodiesel is refined in a simple

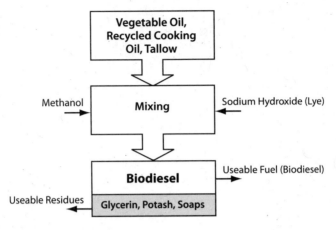

Fig. 12.1: *Simplified biodiesel refining process.*

chemical process called *transesterification,* that removes heavy-viscosity animal fats from source material and results in a purified liquid suitable for use as fuel.

Most modern diesel engines on boats can run on biodiesel without modification. The benefits are significant.

Above is a simplified diagram of the process by which biodiesel is refined.

Did You Know?

• Biodiesel mixes well with regular diesel in blends described as B10, B20, B80, etc. This refers to what percentage of the mixture is biodiesel (e.g., B20 = 20% biodiesel).
• Combusted biodiesel smells like French fries, steak cooking on a grill, hamburgers, popcorn or donuts, depending upon whom you ask.
• The typical "diesel smell" associated with boats is eliminated with biodiesel, resulting in a more pleasant cabin environment and less expenditure on washing and dry-cleaning clothes.
• Biodiesel fuel filter changes do not require gloves.

Engine Benefits from Biodiesel

Biodiesel has a higher cetane number (CN) than petroleum diesel. The CN is a measure of the combustibility of diesel fuel under compression, actually how long after injection the fuel ignites. The higher the CN, the shorter the delay between injection and combustion. Petroleum diesel in the United States generally has a CN between 40 and 46. Biodiesel has a CN over 50.

Biodiesel has no sulfur, yet it possesses high lubricity. EPA regulations have decreased the amount of sulfur in petroleum diesel, and new regulations in both the United States and Canada will result in petroleum diesel fuel with significantly less sulfur, a harmful fuel emission. The process of removing sulfur from petroleum diesel fuel also removes naturally occurring lubricity agents. Many boaters already mix their petroleum diesel with lubricity additives. Not surprisingly, some of those additives are themselves biodiesel.

Health Benefits from Biodiesel

Biodiesel is safer to handle, store and use. The flashpoint of biodiesel (the temperature at which it ignites) is above 400°F (200°C), while the flashpoint of petroleum diesel is about 150°F (70°C). B100 emissions have no by-products that cause mortality cancer, genetic or systemic changes in laboratory animals. Petroleum diesel emissions have by-products that do cause mortality, cancer and other serious biological changes in laboratory animals.

Environmental Benefits from Biodiesel

Just a 20% blend of biodiesel (B20) can help the environment with:

- Decreased contributions to global warming by significantly reducing carbon-based, greenhouse gasses.
- Decreased forest and vegetation destruction through zero emission of sulfur compounds which cause acid rain.
- Decreased toxic emissions that enhance the life cycle of marine and non-marine plants and animals.
- Significantly reduced impact of spill. Biodiesel degrades about four times faster than petroleum diesel after spillage, with most of a spill organically broken down after just 28 days.
- Decreased reliance on fossil fuels.

Drawbacks of Using Biodiesel

Biodiesel generally costs more than petroleum diesel, although with steadily rising oil prices, this may not always be the case. The higher cost of biodiesel may be offset by its other benefits. Even though biodiesel improves engine performance, its use may void some engine warranties. Check with your engine manufacturer and insurer.

Biodiesel is not readily available at marine fuel docks, although this is changing as more boaters ask for biodiesel. Once you begin using biodiesel, you will not want to switch back to regular diesel.

The smell of biodiesel has been known to attract wildlife. In Colorado a black bear attacked the biodiesel pumps at a gas station. Presumably, this won't be a problem for boaters (although grizzly bears are known to swim!).

Biodiesel may not work well in diesel furnaces or diesel stoves. Without the high pressures and high temperatures of combustion, biodiesel may leave a residue that clogs these devices.

Steps You Can Take

Biodiesel is a win-win situation for your health, for your boat and for our environment. Considering converting to biodiesel? Here are some steps you can take:

- Replace any rubber hoses and gaskets. Modern diesel engines no longer use rubber hoses and gaskets, but some older engines may still have them. Biodiesel is a solvent, and it will attack rubber hoses and gaskets. Modern hoses and gaskets are made from synthetic compounds like nitrile that are impervious to a solvent like biodiesel.

- Start with a B20 rather than B100. Because biodiesel is also a solvent and will clean out your entire fuel system, initially you may find yourself changing fuel filters more frequently. Actually this is a good thing that biodiesel helps keep your fuel system — from tank to cylinder — clean. Over time you can upgrade toward B100.

- Use only biodiesel refined to meet ASTM 6751 standards. ASTM is the American Society for Testing and Materials, which maintains standards for the quality of all fuels, including biodiesel. While you can make biodiesel in your kitchen with a blender and readily available chemicals, for your boat's engine only use the highest quality biodiesel.

- Don't be afraid to mix any percentage of biodiesel with the petroleum diesel already in your tank.

- Periodically service your injectors, or add an injector cleansing compound to the fuel.

Getting Biodiesel to Your Boat

Some fuels docks carry biodiesel, but most do not. Here are some tips on getting biodiesel down to your boat:

- Keep biodiesel in a five-gallon jerry can and pour it directly into your fuel tank. Since many ports and marinas do not allow for dockside fueling from a portable can, take the can when you next go to the fuel dock and fuel there.
- Keep jerry cans of biodiesel as your backup fuel source should your tanks run out. Remember biodiesel is safer to handle and store than petroleum diesel.
- Work with local suppliers of biodiesel. They may be able to bring a biodiesel fuel truck to an approved area for fueling at your marina or port, especially if you'll be filling a large tank.
- When you're next hauled out, ask the yard if it's possible for a biodiesel truck to pull alongside your boat and fuel you. Make sure the biodiesel supplier is bonded to deliver fuel this way.
- Lobby your marina, port or fuel dock to install a biodiesel pump.
- Even though biodiesel is an ocean-friendly fuel, treat it as you would any fuel, following safety precautions when filling your tank. (See recommendations in chapter 10.)

Straight Vegetable Oil and Other Biodiesel Fuels

Willie Nelson has run his diesel Mercedes Benz car on 100 percent vegetable oil for several years. The truth is that diesel engines are capable of burning straight vegetable oil, or SVO, as it is known. Diesel engines can also run on used or waste vegetable oil (WVO). The main problem is starting up and shutting down the engine. SVO and WVO are more viscous than biodiesel or petroleum diesel and can clog injectors and injector lines. However, once the engine is running, high internal temperatures prevent such clogging.

A number of different SVO conversion kits are available that provide filters, an auxiliary fuel tank filled with refined biodiesel or petroleum diesel, a monitoring system for engine temperature and a switch that selects whether the engine is running from the auxiliary tank or the main tank filled with SVO. With this system, the engine is started on biodiesel or petroleum diesel. The operator monitors the temperature of the engine and then switches to SVO. Before shutting down the engine, the operator switches back to biodiesel or petroleum diesel. This approach is often coupled with heating the vegetable oil prior to supplying it to the injectors, thereby insuring that a combustible fuel is available. Some conversion kits are computer-based and perform heating and switching between SVO and refined diesel fuel, automatically.

There is absolutely no reason why recreational boat owners cannot install SVO conversion kits on their diesel engines and power their boats using SVO. In fact recreational boat owners have performed this conversion. The process of heating thick oil prior to supplying it to a diesel engine has been used in large ocean-going vessels for decades. On these ships, a thick tar-like oil known as bunker oil is heated then supplied to the ship's main engines, which may be started or stopped on regular petroleum diesel.

Resources

Randall von Wedel. *Technical Handbook for Marine Biodiesel in Recreational Boats.* CytoCulture International, Inc., 2nd Edition, April 22, 1999 (prepared for the National Renewable Energy Laboratory, US Department of Energy): www.cytoculture.com/Biodiesel%20Handbook.htm.

The US National Biodiesel Board (NBB) is a "not-for-profit corporation dedicated to the commercialization and industrialization of biodiesel." It represents agribusiness interests, and its members are large-scale commercial producers. It does not favor small-scale local operations and home-brewers. www.Biodiesel.org/. The NBB maintains one of the best technical databases on biodiesel research (searchable): www.Biodiesel.org/resources/reportsdatabase/.

Journey to Forever. A resource for SVO and WVO conversion with information about the many different options available and pros and cons of each. journeytoforever.org/biodiesel_svo.html.

Internet Search Terms

biodiesel; biodiesel boats; biodiesel marine; "straight vegetable oil" "conversion kits"; SVO diesel engines

CHAPTER 13

Use Ethanol

Know the benefits and harms associated with ethanol.

It would be nice if it were possible to say that as good as biodiesel is for diesel engines, ethanol is for gasoline engines on boats, but it would not be completely truthful. With numerous reports of fuel tank and engine damage from boaters using ethanol-blended gasoline, this biofuel is at the center of a controversy for the marine industry. If you own a gasoline-powered engine, you have a choice about using ethanol, so you need to understand the promises and the pitfalls of this biofuel.

Ethanol is produced by fermenting sugar in the presence of yeast. Yes, the same process that produces the alcohol we consume. In fact ethanol is simply another name for drinking alcohol, or grain alcohol. They are the same chemical compound and can be produced from a wide range of crops, not just corn. When mixed with gasoline, ethanol reduces environmentally harmful by-products of combustion such as carbon monoxide and carbon dioxide, two of many so-called GHGs, or greenhouse gases.

Is Ethanol Really Beneficial to the Environment?

Most ethanol in the United States is produced from corn. Fossil fuels are used in the process of growing corn such as fertilizers, for farm equipment and in the production and transportation of ethanol itself. Some studies have shown that when you factor in all these costs, more energy is spent producing ethanol than gained from burning it — 29% more according to a Cornell University report.[1] Other studies have shown only a modest gain of 25% more energy in burning ethanol over producing it. Compare with studies that show a net gain of 93% when producing and burning biodiesel.[2] Ethanol production is also driving up the cost of food as corn acreage once in production for livestock feed is now being turned into production for ethanol.[3]

Ethanol and Marine Engines

Controversy aside, boaters have to face a number of issues when they pull up to the fuel dock and are forced to put ethanol in their tanks. The problem here is similar to the ones stated above: Does the use of ethanol in marine engines produce greater benefits to the environment than any potential harm it creates?

The Energy Policy Act of 2005 mandated a switch to ethanol from MBTE, a fuel additive shown to be harmful to human health and the environment. Some states are mandating E20 fuel (fuel with 20% ethanol) at all pumps, including marinas.

Ethanol is a solvent that will loosen varnish, rust and particulate matter in the fuel tank, injectors, carburetors and within the engine, sending the sludge throughout the fuel system. It can also attack the resins in fiberglass fuel tanks causing them to fail. The alcohol in ethanol can dry out gaskets, seals and hoses, causing fuel leakage.

Ethanol absorbs more than 10 times the amount of water than MBTE, the fuel additive that it is meant to replace. Ethanol also absorbs moisture in the air even through the vents of a fuel tank, rendering the fuel stratified — a layer of oil atop a layer of water — and unusable. This

MBTE

Methyl tert butyl ethane is a byproduct of petroleum manufacturing used as a replacement for lead in gasoline. Like lead, MBTE helps to reduce "engine knock." It also oxygenates gasoline.

In 1995, high levels of MBTE were discovered in tens of thousands of public and private wells across the US from leakage of underground gasoline storage tanks.

When diluted with groundwater, MBTE reacts to produce carcinogenic substances such as benzene and toluene. By 2004, many states had enacted legislation banning the use of MBTE.

can cause sudden engine shutdown. Ethanol burns less efficiently than MBTE, which it replaces, producing less top RPMs and boat speeds of up to one knot less than with non-ethanol gasoline.

Studies on small engines have shown that E20 increases engine wear and reduces engine life[4] and other effects, including:

- Exhaust temperatures up 100°F
- Peak cylinder pressures higher
- Combustion deposits
- Cylinder head gasket burned and failed
- Exhaust valve burned
- Cylinder bore scored: 25 hours light-duty emissions testing; lost cylinder compression; lost 20% power

Steps You Can Take

- Ask before you pump, "Is this fuel an ethanol blend?" Fuel stations are required to post prominent signs about ethanol-blended gasoline.
- If you have fiberglass fuel tanks, you may need to replace them before first using ethanol.
- Avoid mixing MBTE-blended gasoline with ethanol. The reaction may precipitate out substances that prevent proper engine function. Empty your tanks before switching fuel types.
- Because it absorbs water, ethanol fuel has a very short shelf life compared to non-ethanol gasoline. Limit your fuel onboard to what's needed in the next two weeks.
- Use a good water separator fuel filter and always carry several spare filter cartridges.
- You may need to empty your tank when storing the boat over winter.
- Keep abreast of the latest findings about ethanol and marine engines. (See resources section below)
- Be aware of state efforts to mandate ethanol levels.
- Join marine industry lobbying efforts to produce legislation mandating standards that produce overall gains for the marine environment rather than standards that give with one hand, while taking away with the other. For example, ethanol, while cleaner burning, may produce a higher overall rate of fuel tank failure that results in more fuel spills into bilges and the water than from boats not using ethanol.

Resources

The National Marine Manufacturers Association (NMMA) continually monitors this ethanol issue for boaters. Their website has several good articles on the subject. www.nmma.org/government/environmental/?catid=937

"Deathanol." *Boating Life*: www.boatinglife.com/article_content.jsp?ID=44482

About: Powerboating has a series of articles on ethanol with suggestions to boaters: www.powerboat.about.com/od/maintenance/a/Engines_Ethanol.htm

Internet Search Terms

ethanol controversy; ethanol boats; ethanol "marine engines"

CHAPTER 14

Different Strokes for Different Boats

New technologies provide choices for outboards.

Outboard engines are an essential aspect of modern-day boating. Many sailboats use outboard engines as power when not under sail. Some boats are powered exclusively by outboards. Most boaters use outboards to power their dinghies. Most of these outboard engines, ranging from 1.5 to 300 horsepower, use conventional gasoline engines in a carbureted two-stroke power cycle. Since both the intake and exhaust ports of each cylinder open at the same time, these engines do not completely burn all their fuel. Instead, they release as much as 20% to 30% of partially combusted by-products directly into the air and/or water. Because most two-stroke engines also require oil to be mixed with the fuel prior to combustion, this partially combusted release contains both unburned gasoline and oil.

In 1998 the Environmental Protection Agency stipulated that by 2006 all outboard engines sold in the United States meet a 75% reduction in emissions from uncontrolled levels. This effectively spelled the death of the old, smelly two-stroke, and that's a great thing for boaters because newer technologies have now given us more efficient engines that release fewer pollutants.

A New Breed of Outboards

Boaters now have a choice of four different types of outboard engines. All of these technologies have their advantages and disadvantages, but most importantly, all reduce the environmental impact of using outboard engines.

Direct Fuel Injection Engines. Like their diesel counterparts, two-stroke direct fuel-injection (DFI) engines spray a regulated amount of fuel into each cylinder. At this point in its cycle, the piston is covering the intake and exhaust valves, preventing the release of unburned fuel. Most DFI two-cycle engines still require the addition of oil to the fuel.

Four-Stroke Engines. Four-stroke outboard engines are very similar to the gasoline engines that power modern cars. Since intake and exhaust valves never open at the same time, uncombusted fuel is not released from the cylinder chambers.

Diesel Outboard Engines. Diesel outboard engines make a lot of sense, and a handful of manufacturers produce them. Not only are they more fuel efficient, but they can also easily burn alternative fuels like biodiesel (see chapter 12 on biodiesel). On a diesel boat, a diesel outboard means one less type of fuel to carry, which also reduces fire hazard since gasoline is more flammable than diesel. The drawback of a diesel outboard is its increased weight, necessary to handle the higher temperatures and compression that a diesel engine requires.

Electric Outboard Engines. Electric engines are the no-fuel alternatives, an exciting option for powering vessels of all sizes. They're covered along with hybrid marine engine technology in chapter 15.

Benefits of Four-stroke and Two-stroke DFI Engines

Improved fuel efficiency (25% to 45%) and more complete fuel burn saves money: $2 to $3 out of every $10 spent on fuel for an older two-cycle engine is wasted and ends up in the air and water. DFIs decrease oil consumption by 50%, and less oil is released into the air and water. Four-stroke engines require no oil to be mixed with the fuel. Hydrocarbon emissions are reduced by 75% to 90%.

These engines start more easily under both hot and cold conditions, idle better at low speed (lower vibration/noise), run quieter, reduce the smell of smoke and improve performance with smoother combustion.

Drawbacks of Four-stroke and Two-stroke DFI Engines

Four-stroke and two-stroke DFI engines weigh more than traditional two-cycle outboards, on average 25% greater weight. Newer engines cost more than their older counterparts, although that cost is eventually offset in fuel savings and environmental protection.

Benefits of Diesel Outboards

Diesel outboards get better fuel economy with greater savings, and for dinghies on diesel vessels, only one fuel source is needed for all engines. Being less flammable than gasoline, diesel reduces fire hazard. Biodiesel can be used in diesel outboards for even more benefits (see section on biodiesel).

Drawbacks of Diesel Outboards

Diesel outboards weigh significantly more than their gasoline counterparts and also cost more, although that is eventually offset in fuel savings and environmental protection. These are rarer outboard engines, which may make finding parts and service more difficult.

Internet Search Terms

Biodiesel; Biodiesel boats; Biodiesel marine; "straight vegetable oil" "conversion kits"; svo diesel engines

CHAPTER 15

Electrify Your Boating Experience

Consider electric or hybrid engines for your vessel.

In 1838, Tzar Nicholas I of Russia supported the German physicist Moritz Hermann Jacobi in outfitting a ten-person oar boat with a primitive electric motor and two side paddlewheels, so it could ferry intrepid passengers up the River Neva. In 1848 Benjamin Hill and John Dillwyn Llewellyn demonstrated an electric-powered boat on a lake near Swansea, Wales. In the 1860s Count de Molin experimented with electric paddlewheel boats in the Bois de Bologne in Paris. These early electric boats were cumbersome and often belched as much thick smoke from their huge batteries as locomotives did from burning coal. A breakthrough in electric motor propulsion for boats came between 1880 and 1881 when the Parisian machinist and inventor Gustave Trove designed and patented the first electric outboard engine, weighing 11 pounds, and using a multi-blade propeller.

At the 1893 Chicago World's Fair, the Electric Launch Company (Elco) provided a fleet of 54 boats with inboard electric motors to carry passengers on demonstration trips over a Chicago lake. Early 20th century industrial tycoons William K. Vanderbilt and John Jacob Astor each built electric boats. Astor's vessel, *Utopia*, was 72 feet long and powered by two 25-horsepower electric motors.

Many modern-day boaters are familiar with electric trolling motors that propel smaller fishing boats quietly over inland lakes and waterways. Beyond that, full-fledged electric outboards and powerful hybrid diesel-electric technology is available to power dinghies and vessels up to 60 feet.

If you need to repower your main vessel, or your dinghy, consider an electric power option.

Electric vs. Diesel vs. Gasoline Motors

Electric motors running off batteries are cleaner and smaller, require less maintenance and are pound-for-pound more powerful than their diesel or gasoline counterparts. Most boat owners are used to comparing motors by horsepower — the greater the horsepower, the more power delivered to propel a boat. It then comes as a complete surprise, coupled with a good deal of skepticism, when they hear that an electric motor with a small horsepower rating can propel a vessel at the same speed as a diesel or gasoline motor of much higher horsepower.

David Tether, formerly with Solomon Technologies (developers of electric propulsion systems for sailboats and displacement powerboats), observes:

> We have also found that a high torque motor in a boating application has many benefits over a lower torque motor. This is why, when comparing diesel engines to gasoline engines, the higher torque diesel engine will push a larger, more efficient propeller with less horsepower. The Solomon Technologies, Inc. motor which has even higher torque will push even bigger low RPM props. The operative word is torque. That is what propellers want and Horsepower = RPM x Torque. With this in mind we see that two motors can have the same horsepower, but one is 3,000 RPM and 10 ft/lbs. of torque and the other is 1,000 RPM and 30 ft/lbs of torque.[1]

Hybrid Diesel-Electric Propulsion

Hybrid diesel-electric engines are available for powering sailboats and displacement powerboats at prices comparable to, if not less than, traditional diesel engines. In a typical hybrid system, a powerful electric motor, running off a bank of batteries, drives the shaft. A diesel generator, in turn, charges the battery bank.

Did you know that a diesel generator in a hybrid propulsion system is more efficient than a stand-alone diesel engine used for propulsion?

- A generator is designed to run at a given RPM with a balanced load to make electricity.

- The alternator can be smaller because it is charging batteries only over a long period.
- A generator has no transmission, and therefore much less "parasitic loss" due to gears, shaft and propeller.
- A generator runs at a near constant temperature and therefore can be contained in a heat and sound shield.
- The muffler on a diesel generator is smaller than on a diesel engine used for propulsion.
- Overall effect is for the generator to convert fuel to energy many times more efficiently than a diesel engine used for propulsion, with a significant reduction in moving parts and maintenance.
- Diesel generators can operate on biodiesel, thereby enhancing further the operating efficiency while increasing safety, reducing health hazards and minimizing environmental impact (see chapter 12 on biodiesel).
- Not all hybrid diesel-electric propulsion systems use generators running at a steady rate. Some use sophisticated computer-controlled regulators to alternate generators in and out of service, and regulate the speeds at which they run.

Electric Outboard Engines

Even if your are not repowering your main vessel, or considering the purchase of a new vessel with a hybrid diesel-electric propulsion system, you can still gain the benefits of electric propulsion for your dinghy. Electric outboards range from 2.0 to 9.0 horsepower, some single-construction units, others retrofitted heads to standard

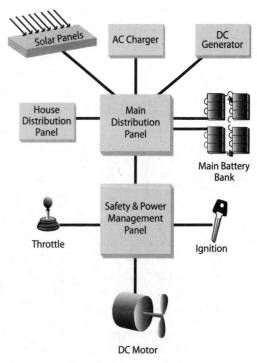

Fig. 15.1: *Basic elements of a diesel-electric hybrid propulsion system*

outboard lower units, with battery life up to several hours depending on the size of the battery bank.

Benefits of Electric Propulsion (Hybrid or Straight)

- High efficiency
- Reliability
- Increased maneuverability at low speeds
- Reduced noise
- Greater safety by eliminating gasoline
- Smoother starting and operation
- Lower maintenance and operating costs
- Zero emissions into water and air
- Electricity from a renewable resource through use of solar panels and wind generators

Resources

Solomon Technologies. Makers of complete hybrid diesel-electric systems for sailboats and displacement powerboats: www.solomontechnologies.com

Ossa Powerlite. Makers of hybrid diesel-electric propulsion systems for boats: www.ossapowerlite.com

Island Pilot. Makers of a diesel-solar-electric hybrid-power catamaran capable of cruising at six knots under solar power alone: www.dsehybrid.com

Ray Electric Outboard. Long-time maker of electric outboards, 2.5, 4.0 and 5.0 hp: www.rayeo.com

Outboard Electric Corp. Makers of a 5.5 hp electric outboard: www.outboardelectric.org

eCycle Marine. Makers of replacement electric power heads for Yamaha 6, 8 and 9.9 hp outboards: www.ecyclemarine.com

Minn Kota. Makers of the eDrive 2 hp electric outboard and a variety of electric trolling motors. www.minnkotamotors.com

Briggs & Stratton. Makers of the eTek 3 hp electric outboard designed for fresh water use only: www.briggsandstratton.com

Internet Search Terms

"hybrid diesel electric" marine, "electric outboard"

CHAPTER 16

Use Your Head to Protect Our Waters

Choose marine sanitation units that help the environment.

L et's put it to rest. "Poop deck," when used in reference to old sailing ships, has nothing to do with bodily functions of a similar name. The poop in question here comes from the Latin *puppis* meaning "stern." The poop deck is actually the flat surface of the roof above a raised aft cabin, which served as a command bridge on older sailing vessels.

"Head," on the other hand, does refer to the toilet on a boat or ship. It comes from the days when the toilet was little more than a hole through the decks at the most forward part of the ship, where natural wake action would carry away human waste, and the wind, which generally came from behind on a sailing vessel, would carry away the smell. Modern day heads are more than just open holes to the sea, but unless they are used, maintained and emptied correctly, they might as well be.

What's wrong with flushing human waste into the vastness of our oceans?

The Impact of Marine Sewage

Marine vessel sewage is much more concentrated than domestic sewage because much less water is used per flush. According to the US Environmental Protection Agency (EPA), the amount of bacterial pollution from one weekend boater's discharge of untreated sewage is equal to the amount from the treated sewage of 10,000 people during the same time period! Sewage contamination is measured in terms of fecal coliform levels — bacteria found in the intestines of all warm-blooded animals. Test results are expressed as the number of bacteria per 100 milliliters (ml) of water. Shellfish beds are closed when the coliform count reaches 14 per 100 ml of water. Public beaches are closed to swimmers when the coliform count reaches 200 per 100 ml of water.

Raw or poorly treated sewage can spread disease. Organic matter in sewage is decomposed by bacteria in the water. During this process, the bacteria use oxygen. As a result, sewage in the water may deplete the water's oxygen level, causing disease and stress to fish and other aquatic animals. Shellfish are filter feeders that eat tiny food particles filtered through their gills into their stomachs, along with bacteria from sewage. They can convey nearly all waterborne pathogens to humans, including hepatitis, typhoid and cholera.

In February 1995, 70 persons in Louisiana, Mississippi, Maryland and North Carolina were sickened with gastroenteritis by a virus after eating raw oysters from a remote oyster bed in Louisiana. The *Journal of the American Medical Association* reported that the outbreak was traced to a specific commercial oyster boat that disposed of its untreated sewage directly overboard. The US Food and Drug Administration was able to trace this outbreak to one individual mariner because the virus samples from each affected person had the same DNA sequence.

The 1, 2, 3s of Marine Sanitation

What exactly is a marine sanitation device? The Federal Water Pollution Act (Clean Water Act) defines a marine sanitation device as "any equipment for installation on board a vessel which is designed to receive, retain, treat or discharge sewage, and any process to treat such sewage." So any equipment from your toilet proper to your holding tank, and from your holding tank to your on-deck pump-out fitting is considered a marine sanitation device or MSD. The definition is a bit misleading, since under it, a piece of hose and a macerator pump would both be considered MSDs, since one receives sewage and the other treats it. It's best, then, to treat your entire sewage system — from toilet to tank, from tank to pump-out fitting — as a single MSD.

All recreational boats with installed toilet facilities must have an operable MSD on board. Vessels 65 feet and under may use a Type I, II or III MSD. Vessels over 65 feet must install a Type II or III MSD. All installed MSDs must be Coast Guard certified. Coast Guard certified devices are so labeled except for some holding tanks, which are certified by definition under the regulations. Vessels smaller than 26 feet and without sleeping accommodations are not required to have operable marine sanitation devices, but if they do have a portable waste removal system, such as portable potties, those systems must be operated within applicable federal and state guidelines. The three types of MSDs are defined as:

Type I MSD. A flow-through treatment system that disinfects fecal coliform bacteria to no more than 1,000 parts per 100ml and discharges no visible floating solids.

Type II MSD. A flow-through treatment system that disinfects fecal coliform bacteria to no more than 200 parts per 100ml and discharges no more than 150mg per liter of suspended solids. The discharge from a Type II MSD is a clear, though not necessarily colorless, liquid.

Type III MSD. A holding tank that performs no treatment, but simply holds waste material for pump-out into a shore-based facility. Any holding tank, including a porta-potty, would by definition be considered a Type III MSD.

Protecting the Marine Environment Doesn't Have to Stink

The truth is that your boat's head does not have to stink ... really! Many boaters have heard that sewage-saturated hoses are the cause of the foul odors that emanate from their sanitation system. But hoses are just one part of the equation for the smells associated with human waste removal aboard a boat — and a very small part in modern-day marine sanitation systems. To understand where the smells in a marine sanitation system come from, it helps to know the natural cycle of waste breakdown.

When waste sits in your holding tank (a Type III MSD), two different kinds of organisms act upon it to break it down: aerobic and anaerobic bacteria. These organisms require completely different environments and compete to drive each other out. Aerobic bacteria require oxygen to live and function. Anaerobic require an environment free of oxygen. In fact, anaerobic bacteria are killed in the presence of oxygen. This is important because it is the anaerobic bacteria in your holding tank that produce a variety of noxious compounds: sulfur oxides (rotten egg smell), methane, which has no odor but is flammable, and carbon dioxide beneficial for anaerobic bacteria but lethal to aerobic bacteria. To oversimplify the matter: aerobic bacteria are the good guys of your holding tank, anaerobic bacteria are the bad guys.

Most of the tank enzymes that boaters add to their holding tanks do little if anything. Chemical products hide one odor with another odor. Furthermore, they kill both anaerobic and beneficial aerobic bacteria, thus producing more problems than they solve. In the event that you need to pump overboard, many of these chemical additives are extremely harmful to the environment. The key to an odor-free sanitation system is simple, though counterintuitive: make sure that you have good airflow into the system, which will eliminate the anaerobic bacteria, and remove any carbon dioxide that they create.

Different Kinds of Holding Tank Treatments

"Holding tank" smell can drive boaters to distraction, and the expense of buying products to eliminate it. Most often, these products do little more than cover up the smell. Sometimes they actually make matters worse by eliminating beneficial bacteria in the holding tank through introducing harsh, toxic chemicals. If you are going to use a chemical treatment for your holding tank, here are some things you should know about the four treatment methods[1]:

1. **Chemical treatments,** the most common, kill bacteria immediately. They very effectively control odors by masking smells with deodorant. Although relatively inexpensive, chemicals must be added regularly. They are not designed to dissolve waste, and they are the least environmentally friendly. And some deodorants use formaldehyde or bromine, which are toxic to both humans and the marine environment.

2. **Enzyme treatments** accelerate the digestion of organic materials in waste and neutralize odors at the same time. They work quickly to completely emulsify paper and sewage and have extremely low toxicity. They must be added regularly and have a limited range of effectiveness in terms of temperature and pH. Enzymes require a tank free from residuals of other treatment products.

3. **Nitrate treatments** provide an interesting but expensive alternative. Oxygen is vital to bacteria in the process of breaking down organic waste. When little air is present, as in most holding tanks, bacteria derive the oxygen from sulfates in the waste,

which produces hydrogen sulfide (stinky!) gas. When nitrates are introduced, they act as nutrients for the bacteria, providing an alternative source of oxygen, which results in the production of nitrogen (odorless) gas. Environmentally friendly nitrates speed up the breakdown process and eliminate odors. They require a tank free of the residuals from other products.

4. **Bioactive treatments** contain live aerobic bacteria, which break down waste, reproduce and crowd out anaerobic (odor-producing) bacteria. They, too, are environmentally friendly. Like enzymes, bioactive treatments emulsify paper and sewage completely. Unlike other treatments, they multiply and continue to work long after treatment is complete, eliminating the need to add more between pump-outs. To survive, however, the microbes require a well-ventilated holding tank, free of residuals. Although initially expensive, bioactive treatments become more cost effective over time because of bacteria propagation.

Steps You Can Take

- Make sure your holding tank system has adequate air flow. Eliminate any low spots in vent lines that would restrict the flow of air.
- Avoid the use of detergent, bleach, dish soap or other cleaners or odor-masking agents in the holding tank.
- If you feel you must use a holding tank additive, use a formaldehyde- and bromine free additive that provides aerobic bacteria to the tank.
- Change the hoses, seals, gaskets and impellers in your sanitation system on a regular basis.
- Always pump-out when you can. (See the next section on pumping-out.)

Alternative Heads

One alternative to traditional MSDs that boaters can use for marine sanitation is the dry head or composting toilet. First, it's probably not a good idea to think about a composting toilet on your boat in the same way you think about the compost pile in your backyard. There, food waste is disposed of, and a combination of bacteria and earthworms break down the refuse into usable nutrients that can be applied to plants and vegetables. Let's be clear on this: We're not talking about growing vegetables aboard from the products of your sanitation system, even if that were technically feasible.

What is important to recognize is that almost 90 percent of human waste is liquid. When that liquid is evaporated, what remains is a dry compost material. Dry heads accomplish this by heater elements and fans to remove moisture in the air of the tank. Some dry heads also separate urine from fecal material, thereby further reducing the volume of sewage held in the main tank. The principal environmental concern is with human feces, not urine, since urine is most often sterile, while feces contain a variety of harmful pathogens.

Advantages of Dry Heads

- Less frequent emptying of holding tank. In the absence of liquid, the volume held in the unit's holding tank is greatly reduced.
- No need to use a pump-out facility. The end-product of a dry head is compostible material that can be disposed of on land in a flower garden, municipal compost bin or any place that compost material can be legally disposed of.
- No odor. Properly fitted with a fan and heating unit, dry heads should have no odor at all.
- Uses less space. Most dry heads have their holding tank built into the base of the unit, eliminating the remote tank needed on traditional MSDs.
- Ease of installation. All that's needed is the toilet, a vent to the outside and an electrical connection for the fan and heater. No hoses, valves, clamps, tanks, pumps, etc. Most manufacturers recommend leaving the fan running continuously, even when the boat is not in use. Install a small solar cell to offset the fan's electrical drain.
- Reduced maintenance. With fewer parts to a dry head, comes less maintenance and fewer frequent breakdowns.
- Environmentally friendly. Eliminates the need for harmful chemicals to mask odors.
- Reduced cost. Dry heads typically cost much less than conventional Type I or Type II MSDs.

Resources
See the list of Internet Search Terms, which will lead you to a wealth of information on traditional marine sanitation units and alternative units such as dry heads.

Internet Search Terms
"marine sanitation devices", "marine composting toilet", "MSD marine"

CHAPTER 17

Use a Pump-out Facility Whenever Possible

Pumping-out contributes to human health and
the health of our waters.

From shore, a black bear eyed me as I turned to port at Okisollo Channel north of Quadra Island, British Columbia, and headed toward Upper and Lower Rapids. I checked the time; in an hour the rapids would turn to slack. I threaded the narrow passage between reefs to enter Owen Bay. There, waiting for slack, I reread my cruising guide several times. Don't be fooled, it said. The rapids have sucked boaters in dinghies into their swift currents and to their death. I waited. A 50-foot vessel cruised out of Owen Bay, bow proud, challenging the swirling waters. It charged ahead, and effortlessly the waters threw it back. Again and again, the vessel struck at the rapids. But this jousting match was uneven. Each time, the water had its way. Finally, the vessel turned back, and chastened, headed to Owen Bay to wait with me.

Shortly before slack, we both headed out and made our way with ease past Lower Rapids, then Hole-in-the-Wall, another fast-water chute. At the confluence of these rapids, I turned to starboard, heading into the Octopus Islands and wended my way through a maze of rocks and islets until reaching Waiatt Bay in the center of this rocky warren. There, in a huge bay, surrounded by lush foothills, at least 70 other boats lay at anchor. I chose a spot in a far corner of the bay. With my anchor set, I stepped out onto the rear deck to enjoy the day.

The Clean Vessel Act

In 1992, the United States Congress passed the Clean Vessel Act (CVA), not to be confused with the Clean Water Act (CWA). The Act was meant to assist States and marinas in helping to provide more adequate pumpout facilities for recreational boaters through a $40 million federal grant program administered by the US Fish and Wildlife Service. The CVA was extended in 1998 with Congress providing an additional $50 million to help boaters find alternatives to pumping overboard.

No sooner had I sat down, than I nearly gagged. The over-powering stench of human waste filled the air. Boaters freely pumped their holding tanks into the bay, turning these calm waters into a summer's cesspool. Saddened and angry, I weighed anchor and headed toward less-polluted waters.

But the effect of dumping raw sewage into the sea is much greater than destroying the pristine beauty of favorite anchorage. As described in the last chapter, sewage can have disastrous effects on the health of humans and the oceans.

Steps You Can Take

- Keep a chart of pump-out facilities handy for the areas that you cruise. Enter their locations as markers on your GPS or computer navigational system.
- Learn to use the pump-out station at your local marina. Thanks to the Clean Vessel Act, many marinas have upgraded their pump-out facilities in the past several years. State-of-the-art pump-out stations are quick and efficient. Ask your marina or port facility to show you the proper way to use their stationary or portable pump-out stations. If you belong to a boating group or association, turn this instructional lesson into an outing for the entire club.
- Only pump out your sewage holding tank at a pump-out station, unless that station is specifically designated to handle other pumping-out duties, such as your boat's bilge. Pumping a bilge into a system not designed to handle it could contaminate the waste removal system.
- Turn off the pump once you're finished.
- Upgrade the Marine Sanitation Device aboard your vessel (see section on Marine Sanitation Devices).

- Know the location of all "no-discharge zones" in the areas that you cruise.

No Pump-outs, Now What?

Boaters often find themselves in areas where there are no pump-out facilities, and they must empty their heads overboard. Even in that situation there are measures you can take to protect the marine environment.

Steps You Can Take

- Use common sense. Regardless of signs or posted regulations, the basic idea is to discharge your waste in a way that minimizes contact with human and marine life.
- Under no circumstances discharge your head overboard in no-discharge zones (NDZs) or zero-liquid discharge zones (ZLDs) or aquaculture areas whether signs are posted or not.
- Avoid discharging your head overboard in marine protected areas (MPAs), national wildlife reserves (NWRs) and other marine animal sanctuaries.
- Avoid discharging your head in front of beaches or in water that flows toward a populated area.
- Seek out faster-moving water to discharge your head in, tidal rapids, fast-moving portions of rivers or streams. This will help to disperse your waste and not allow it to concentrate in one area, leading to a potential buildup of pollutants and the beginning of eutrophication.
- If you know you will be cruising in areas without pump-out facilities, eliminate or reduce your use of head treatment chemicals, since these chemicals will be pumped directly into the water.
- If you are aware of areas that other boaters frequently use to pump-out their heads, avoid them. Regular use of a given area leads to eutrophication and the creation of dead zones.

Internet Search Terms

"marine sanitation devices", "marine composting toilet", "MSD marine"

CHAPTER 18

A Gray Area of Protecting Our Waters

Boaters need sensible laws and better technology
to manage gray water.

G ray water is defined as waste water from bathing, laundry and other cleaning, such as washing dishes. The Clean Water Act does not consider gray water as sewage, and thus it is not subject to regulation under this law, even though it is one of the largest sources of liquid discharge from recreational vessels. Gray water frequently contains caustic chemicals such as soaps, detergents and bleaches that can harm the marine environment. Some gray water may also contain bacterial contaminants.

To further complicate matters, some states consider gray water as "sewage" and regulate it as such. In those states, soap bubbles on the water's surface are a reportable pollution offense equivalent to dumping oil overboard. Yet few boats have gray water management systems, especially smaller recreational craft. And plumbing a boat's gray water discharge into its black-water holding tank would quickly overwhelm the capacity of a small boat's Type III MSD system.

Many marinas and other regulatory authorities are mandating Zero Liquid Discharge zones (ZLDs), and it seems clear that this is where pollution management is heading. Still, not all pump-out stations are equipped to handle both black and gray water. Special gray water pump-out stations are sometimes required for boaters that do store their gray water in holding. Until the marine industry gives boaters

Biological Oxygen Demand

When gray water, or black water, enters rivers, lakes and oceans it carries suspended organic substances which must be broken down by bacteria. These bacteria need oxygen to do their work. BOD, or biochemical oxygen demand, describes how much additional demand for oxygen is required by the contaminant that has entered the water. The higher the BOD for breaking down the contaminant, the less available oxygen there is for normal aquatic plants and animals. As the oxygen level approaches zero, greater and greater numbers of species die off.

better technological options to manage ZLD aboard their craft, gray water discharge will remain a gray area. However, there are some promising technologies to deal with gray water and some simple things boaters can do to reduce the impact of their gray water discharge on the marine environment.

The Impact of Gray Water

Gray water discharges increase biochemical oxygen demand (BOD) and lower dissolved oxygen in water. They also increase nutrients in the water, contributing to overpopulation of some aquatic species, such as certain algae, and thus to eutrophication and dead zones. Gray water frequently contains detergents, soaps, bleaches and the residue of cleaning products that are harmful to the marine environment. Gray water from laundry may also contain bacteria and viruses that are harmful to human beings.

Gray water Treatment Technology

Gray water capture and recycling systems have been designed for onboard use, but they have not been a high priority for the recreational marine industry and do not offer many options for boaters. These systems take gray water in holding tanks and use it to flush marine heads, a recycling that is not without its drawbacks. Caustic elements in gray water can damage MSD parts. These noxious chemicals also decrease oxygen in MSD holding tanks, thereby eliminating beneficial aerobic bacteria and helping anaerobic bacteria to flourish, with their accompanying production of foul odors.

Gray water purification systems also have been built, but currently none are commercially available for recreational vessels. As the maritime community approaches a time of ZLD, demand for gray water treatment options may spur their development.

Perhaps the most simple and readily available gray water treatment for boats comes from the ideas behind dry or composting heads. More than 95 percent of gray water is simply water. Thus, evaporating the water makes sense as a means of treating gray water, and such evaporation units are available for boats. As with dry heads, all that is required is a holding tank, a heater and ventilation to the outside. Currently, the only drawback with these units for marine application is that they are designed for vessels with holding tanks of 55 gallons or more. Here again, mandated ZLD may push manufacturers of gray water evaporation units to design smaller systems for the recreational boating market.

Steps You Can Take

Even in the absence of good options for gray water management, you can take a number of steps to mitigate the effect of any gray water discharge from your boat on the marine environment.

- Use shoreside facilities when you're at dock (restrooms, showers, laundry) to reduce gray water generation.
- Minimize your use of sinks, soaps and detergents.
- Rinse your vessel with clean water only.
- Use more environmentally friendly soaps or alternative cleaning products (see chapter 30 on alternate cleaning products).
- Use low-flow shower heads and on-demand sink nozzles.
- If possible, contain your gray water and dispose of it at pump-out stations. Check first with the pump-out station operator to make certain that gray water disposal is acceptable.
- Use sink screens or strainers and dispose of strained waste in the garbage.

Internet Search Terms
"gray water pollution"; "biochemical oxygen demand"; marine "gray water management"; marine "gray water treatment"; "zero-liquid discharge"

CHAPTER 19

Prevent Onboard Fires

Reduce the risks to your crew and the environment.

S eeing flames aboard your boat is one of the most frightening scenarios a boater can imagine. Each year hundreds of boats have onboard fires, some burning to the waterline and sinking. Fire prevention has long been an obsession with boaters. In fact, "Charlie Noble," a nautical term many boaters are familiar with, has its origin in maritime fire prevention. In the 1850s, Charles Noble, a British merchant captain, insisted that the brass/copper galley smokestack be cleaned and polished every day to reduce the fire hazard. Eventually the smokestack itself became known by this captain's name. To reduce the risk of fire, cooks on old wooden ships periodically fired a pistol with buckshot up the smokestack to dislodge the soot and tar, a practice they called "shooting Charlie Noble."

Fortunately, fire prevention aboard vessels has progressed markedly since the days of Charlie Noble. Still, modern-day vessels have many potential sources of fire, undreamed of in bygone days. Fiberglass, the principal construction material of most recreational boats, is a fuel source equal to, if not greater than, wood. Many boaters do not realize that resins like vinyl ester, used in fiberglass boat construction, are petroleum derivatives — basically oil. That's why the construction method is called Fiberglass Reinforced Plastic (FRP). Once ignited, a fiberglass boat can be consumed more rapidly by fire than denser wood and can burn quickly to the waterline. While a wood fire may spread ashes over the water, along with petroleum from any ruptured tanks, a

91

Fig. 19.1: *Fire triangle*

Exploded view of a tetrahedron, or three-sided pyramid

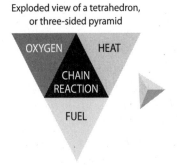

Fig. 19.2: *Fire pyramid*

fiberglass fire always produces an oil slick as it is consumed and rendered back into petroleum.

Most modern boat manufacturers impregnate the resins they use in fiberglass construction with fire retardant substances. Still, the responsibility for fire prevention aboard a boat rests with individual mariners.

The Fire Triangle

Many of us grew up learning the basics of fire prevention through a simple model, the Fire Triangle, that describes the three essential elements of a fire — fuel, heat and oxygen — and shows that removing any of these elements will prevent or arrest a fire.

The Fire Pyramid

More recently, fire experts have suggested an updated fire model, the fire pyramid or fire tetrahedron that depicts the essential elements more accurately. According to this newer model, what was missing from the fire triangle is the chemical chain reaction that sustains the fire. Even in the presence of fuel, oxygen and heat, without a sustaining chemical reaction, a fire will not proceed. This is important for boaters to know because halon and other fire-suppression agents used aboard vessels act to interfere with the chemical reactions between the legs of the fire triangle.

What Causes Boat Fires

AC and DC wiring and appliances account for 55% of boat fires: DC shorts/wiring accounts for 30%; DC engine regulator for 12%; shore power problems for 4%. Wire chafe is the biggest problem for all of these causes. Engine/transmission overheating accounts for 24% of boat fires, mostly due to obstructed intake or exhaust-cooling water passages. Fuel leaks account for a further 8%, with fuel lines, fuel connections on the engine itself and leaking tanks the main culprits.

Steps You Can Take

- Maintain Situational Awareness aboard your vessel (see chapter 8 on Situational Awareness)
- Periodically check wiring for chafe and deterioration. Replace worn wiring.
- Make certain you have a main battery on/off switch and similar switch for your shore power connection. Electrical fires can reignite after being extinguished if electricity is still flowing through wires.
- Regularly inspect and clean exhaust manifolds and risers to prevent them from becoming obstructed and overheating the engine.
- Inspect and change impellers within the cooling system.
- Keep oil and grease out of bilges.
- Clean up any spilled fuel or lube oil immediately and properly dispose of it ashore.
- Stow cleaning materials off the boat.
- Keep all areas free of waste material.
- Use proper containers for flammable liquids.
- Be alert for suspicious odors and fumes, and vent all spaces thoroughly before starting engine(s).
- Turn off your propane solenoid first. Then let burners on stove die before turning stove knobs off.
- Always check all burners are off before turning one on to light the stove.
- Keep propane tanks in cockpit locker that vents overboard.
- Cook remains in/near galley whenever stove is on, especially near if it's on low heat.

ABCs of Fire

Fires are categorized by the kind of material they are using for fuel. This is broken down into four types:

A: Wood, paper, plastic, cloth, rubber

B: Flammable liquids, grease, paint

C: Electrical wiring, fuses, etc.

D: Combustible metals such as sodium, potassium, magnesium, titanium

- Gasoline tanks are kept tied on the deck.
- Run all gasoline out of the outboard before storing it on the cockpit rail.
- Once a month check smoke alarm is functioning OK.
- Turn on the CO_2 detector whenever the engine is running.
- Oily cloths (or those used with flammable liquids, polishes, paints, etc.) should be discarded after use — never keep them in an airtight bag/container. To keep for continued use another day, put them in an open bucket on the deck or in the cockpit.
- Run the blower in the engine room after any propane is exhausted from the stove by mistake.
- Fill the gas tanks on the dock and not on the boat.
- During routine maintenance, inspect the condition of all wiring running through the place where you are working.
- Close the hatches and portholes on the windward side of the boat when refueling.
- No smoking onboard.
- How many fire extinguishers should you carry aboard? Take the Coast Guard requirements for a vessel your size and double them! (See chapter 7 for Coast Guard regulations.)
- Service extinguishers annually.
- Acquaint everyone onboard with the location of all ABC extinguishers and the fire blanket.

Perform Regular Leak Tests of Your Propane System

One time-honored method of checking for a propane leak involves swabbing propane fittings and lines with a soapy liquid and watching for bubbles. An even simpler, and perhaps more effective, method is:

1. Turn off all propane appliances.
2. Turn on the propane solenoid.
3. Open the valve on your propane tank until your system is fully pressurized.
4. Read the pressure from the gauge on the propane tank.
5. Wait five minutes.
6. Read the pressure from the propane tank gauge.
7. If the pressure has dropped more than 3-5 psi, you have a leak!

8. To check if the leak is in the line between the propane tank and the solenoid, close the solenoid, open the tank valve and let the system repressurize. Wait five minutes. If the pressure drops, the leak is between the tank and the solenoid valve.

9. To check if the leak is between the solenoid valve and your appliances, open the solenoid, repressurize the system with propane, then close the solenoid. Wait five minutes, and if the pressure drops, the leak is down the line from the valve.

10. If both steps 8 and 9 show a drop in pressure, the problem might be with a faulty solenoid valve.

Halon and the Environment

Halon 1301 is a compound consisting of bromine, chlorine and fluorine. At high temperatures, halons decompose to release halogen atoms that combine readily with active hydrogen atoms, quenching flame-propagation reaction even when adequate fuel, oxygen and heat remains (see the Fire Pyramid).

For many years, halon was recognized as the firefighting agent of choice aboard vessels. It quickly extinguished all classes of fires. Leaving no residue, it was safe and effective for use around expensive electronic equipment. And halon could be used safely in unoccupied spaces, as well as areas occupied by humans.

But bromine, one of the main ingredients of halon, poses a significant threat to the environment because it promotes depletion of the ozone layer. After December 31, 1993 no new halon could be manufactured in the US. However, recycled or previously manufactured halon is still legal and available for purchase in the US.

You do not have to dispose of your current halon unit. It only poses a danger to the ozone layer if it develops a leak. As long as your unit is in good working condition and not leaking, it's safe and legal to keep aboard. Still, there are now good alternatives that pose a significantly reduced threat to depletion of the ozone layer.

Halon Alternatives

FE-241 and FM-200 are two substances developed to replace halon 1301. FE-241, Chlorotetrafluoroethane, is manufactured by DuPont. FM-200, Heptafluoropropane, is manufactured by the Great Lakes

Chemical Corporation. Both FE-241 and FM-200 have been shown to be relatively safe for people, equipment and the environment. Although both agents do contribute to ozone layer depletion, their contributions are significantly less than halon's. Both of these new agents have a relatively short atmospheric lifetime (somewhere between 7 and 42 years) and, therefore, a minimal direct contribution to global warming.

Did You Know?

- FM-200 is considered to be safe for use in occupied spaces, whereas, FE-241 is not as safe.
- FE-241 is significantly less expensive than FM-200.
- Both require more agent by weight than halon 1301 did, so your storage requirements for the extinguishers may increase.
- Both are Factory Mutual (FM) and USCG approved.

Internet Search Terms

"marine fire prevention", "marine fire safety", "vessel fire prevention," "vessel fire safety," halon, FE-241, FM-200

CHaPTeR 20

Use Radar Prudently

Radar makes for safer boating.

R adar is an essential feature of safe boating. The introduction of low-cost radar units has enabled their use on most small craft, allowing boaters to travel safely in conditions such as heavy fog and darkness. But radar emits non-ionizing radio frequency (RF) radiation. An exposure rate of 3 mg (milligauss) per hour of RF is considered safe by conservative means. Small boat radar is given out in very short bursts so that a unit with a peak power rating of 8,000 watts has an average power rating under 4 watts. While no specific health risks have been associated with small boat radar — and there is no cause for alarm — minimizing direct exposure to this source of electromagnetic radiation is considered prudent. You can reduce your RF exposure from radar through proper installation and operation of your radar unit.

Radar is not the only source of RF aboard your boat (see Table 20.1). We constantly expose ourselves to many sources. One hour of use of these items exposes the user to the following amount of RF.

Steps You Can Take

- Check that your radar is mounted as high as possible on a mast or

Radio frequency exposure from common appliances.

ITEM	EXPOSURE
Mobile phone on standby	90 mg.
Mobile phone in talk mode	1500 mg.
15" computer CRT screen	400 mg.
Small to medium microwave oven (even as much as six feet from the door)	1500 mg.
Power tools and hair driers	600 mg.

Table. 20.1

radar arch. Exposure to RF decreases exponentially with distance from the source.

- Never mount radar so that it transmits within a few feet of a person in the same horizontal plane.
- Periodically check that the radome is moving and not "stuck" in one position while transmitting.
- Don't stand within a few feet of your radar transmitter.
- If you are operating your vessel from the flybridge and do not have a radar screen there, place your radar in standby mode.
- When entering a harbor or at dock, place your radar in standby mode or shut it off. There's no need for radar within a harbor, and there's no need to paint individuals onshore with RF radiation. Some people claim exposure to small boat radar causes them headaches; others say they can hear annoying high-pitched tones.
- Research is still continuing on the health risks of low-level non-ionizing radiation. The International Committee on Electromagnetic Safety (ICES), a subcommittee of the Institute of Electrical and Electronics Engineers, has a standing committee responsible for conducting research and developing standards on RF exposure from small boat radars.
- Be prudent with your radar. Reduce exposure to RF radiation from radar for crew and guests. If you don't need it, don't beam it.

Resources

AMSEA. *Marine Safety Update*. "Electromagnetic Radiation on Boats: Is It Harmful?" Summer 2000: www.amsea.org/pdf/v16n2.pdf

www.microwavenews.com. An online newsletter with information and updates on RF radiation and safety issues.

Internet Search Terms

"small boat radar" exposure; "rf exposure"; "electromagnetic field" exposure

CHAPTER 21

Recycle Underway

We recycle at home, why not on the water?

It's surprising how many boaters who think nothing of separating trash and garbage for recycling in their home forget to do the same while underway. Even though garbage disposal in coastal and inland waters is prohibited, recycling underway adds a measure of protection for the marine environment. Furthermore, when you're back on land, the recyclable waste you dispose of will stay out of landfills and incinerators, thereby further benefiting the environment. With many boaters performing their own oil changes and pumping out their bilges, mariners also have items to dispose of that homeowners usually don't.

Steps You Can Take

Make it a motto to bring back whatever you take out:

- Place at least three separate bins aboard for collection of organic waste, recyclable glass and plastic, and paper.
- Avoid dumping anything overboard, even organic waste. Although organic waste will break down readily, if everyone disposed of their organic refuse in this way, it would quickly overwhelm the ability of organisms and creatures in our waters to decompose it. The breakdown of organic material also requires bacteria, which require oxygen, that deplete oxygen from the water. (See chapter 2.)
- Never discard fishing line, Styrofoam, plastics, cigarette butts or any other trash into the water. Plastics, Styrofoam and cigarette butts

take a long time to break down in the marine environment and are harmful to seabirds and other marine creatures.

- Recycle used fishing line so it doesn't find its way into the water where it can foul props and kill fish.
- Minimize the chance of trash accidentally flying overboard by reducing the amount of trash you bring on board. Buy products that use less packaging. Remove additional packaging from products before you take them onto your boat. When trash accidentally falls overboard, go back and get it (if it is safe to do so).
- Use reusable containers whenever possible. Try to buy in bulk to reduce the amount of packaging you need to discard. Choose products sold in recycled and recyclable containers.
- Recycle your own oil containers by keeping them around to collect the used oil from your next oil change.
- Dump waste oil, waste bilge water and waste fuel in approved facilities at your marina, or in other approved local toxic disposal areas. Have the telephone number of the nearest toxics disposal area available on your boat along with the hours it's open. Plan your times of oil changes and bilge cleaning to coincide with the availability of a location to handle your toxic waste.
- Let paint cans dry thoroughly before disposing of them in the trash.
- If there's a marine exchange store in your area, take anything of value there before placing it in a dumpster. You'll be surprised that other boaters will consider your junk treasure.
- And when you're looking to buy equipment or perform construction on your boat, also visit your local marine exchange. You'll be surprised at what treasures you find there among other boaters' junk, while helping to recycle products that might have wound up in a landfill.
- If you're changing old electronic and computer equipment for newer ones, don't throw the old equipment into the trash bin. Check with a local recycling service to see if they have a program for disposing of electronic equipment.

If you shrink-wrap your boat during the off-season, that large piece of plastic needs to be recycled. The Environment and Plastics Industry Council of Canada recommends that you:

- Ask your port or marina about its shrink-wrap recycling program. If it doesn't have one, ask if they would establish one.
- Remove all rope, strapping, wood frames, doors, zippers and other nonshrink plastic materials.
- Roll the shrink-wrap into a bundle of about five feet long (like a sleeping bag) and tie it with a strip of the shrink-wrap. This helps avoid contamination from other materials.
- If the shrink-wrap is cut just above the horizontal belly band, all of the string will separate instantly. Dispose of this string in a regular dumpster.
- Keep the shrink-wrap dry and clean — no mud, rainwater, leaves, etc.

While in the marina, don't dispose of fish remains by simply tossing them back into the water. Some marinas have policies against this and specific sites for the disposal of fish remains. In Canada, it is illegal to dispose of fish remains in the littoral zone, the area between high and low tides. It's tempting to think that crabs and other bottom-dwellers will recycle these. But in a marina where many people fish, and the water quality is already poor enough that many aquatic species have been driven off, dumping fish entrails into the water simply provides more nutrients that further deplete oxygen levels and degrade the marine environment. Consider freezing whatever fish remains you can and using them for crab bait.

Internet Search Terms
recycling boats; boat "shrink wrap" recycling

FOR THE UPKEEP AND MAINTENANCE OF YOUR VESSEL

MARY JANE JESSEN

CHAPTER 22

Let Your Engine and the Environment Breathe

A crankcase ventilation system has many benefits.

N ormally, in a running diesel or gasoline engine, a small amount of air escapes from each cylinder after compression. This is called blowby. As pistons or valve guides wear, the amount of blowby increases. Blowby carries with it gases of combustion and traces of oil. Most engines release blowby fumes from the crankcase and feed them back into the air-intake system. But as blowby increases, the amount of oil in the blow-by mist also increases and settles over the engine block and throughout the engine room. Oil mist from blowby also runs down the sides of the engine block into the bilge. Oil mist and exhaust gases from blowby make for a dirty engine, a dirty and unhealthy engine room, an oily bilge, potentially unhealthy cabin air and release harmful fumes into the environment.

Consider installing a crankcase ventilation system (CCVS). This simple, non-mechanical system captures blowby gases from the crankcase, and then feeds them through a filter, which separates the oil from the gases. Filtered gases are returned to the air-intake for combustion. Some systems separate the oil and return it to the crankcase. In those systems

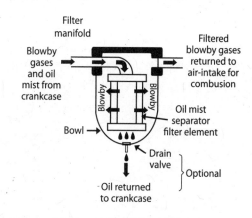

Fig. 22.1: *Diagram of a crankcase ventilation system*

that don't return separated oil, it must be dumped from the unit periodically. Recycle your blowby!

Benefits from a CCVS

A properly installed CCVS can remove up to 99% of the oil mist and airborne particles from the blowby fumes, eliminating their escape into the atmosphere where they would contribute to the deterioration of air quality throughout the vessel. It also reduces oil in the bilge and the chance of oil leakage in bilge water discharge.

By using blowby fumes in combustion, engines (especially older ones) perform better: less oil consumption, less soot and less engine wear.

Steps You Can Take

To determine if you need a CCVS:

- Look for soot in the engine room, particularly around the air-intake and crankcase breather ports.
- Look for oil leaking down the engine near the air intake and breather ports
- Some newer engines come with a CCVS attached or built-in.

If you need a CCVS, choose the one best suited for your engine. CCVSs are made for diesel and gas engines. Manufacturers' guidelines will help determine which size will fit your engine. If you already have a CCVS on your engine, make sure you change the filter periodically.

Resources

Parker-Racor makes crankcase ventilation filter systems in four sizes for diesel engines: www.racor.com. Follow the links to the Marine section.

Walker-Airsep: www.walkerairsep.com. Walker makes a large variety of crankcase ventilation units.

Fleetguard/Nelson Engineering: www.fleetguard.com. Nelson makes the EcoVent® Re-Circulator for diesel engines.

Condensator: www.condensator.com. Condensator makes and markets a family of CCVS units for diesel and gas engines called The CONDENSATOR. Approved for use under California's strict air quality standards, these units do not recycle separated oil, which the company claims benefits the engine by not reintroducing contaminated oil into the crankcase.

Internet Search Terms

"crankcase ventilation" engines; blowby engines; "closed crankcase"

CHAPTER 23

A Boat Green Oil Change

Implement a zero-spill policy for every oil change.

It's one of the messiest jobs we have to do. Yet, to keep an engine running in top shape, engine oil needs to be changed on a regular basis. Along with fueling your main engines or your dinghy's outboard, changing other fluids or cleaning the bilge, changing oil is one of the times when spills happen. Planning an oil change and taking preventative measures beforehand can go a long way toward spill reduction and a less messy oil change. Below are some guidelines you can follow.

Steps You Can Take

Implement a policy of zero-spill for each oil change you perform. That means no spills into your boat, your bilge or the water. Plan your oil change when you know your marina's oil recycling facilities will be available to you, or when state or local oil recycling facilities are open. Winding up with a bucket full of used engine oil with no place to recycle it is a recipe for disaster.

Lay out everything you need beforehand. Don't wait until you're in the middle of the oil change with oil dripping down an old oil filter to realize the new filter is still in the back of your car. Have a spill prevention kit nearby during the oil change, just in case you need it. (See chapter 11 on making a spill prevention kit). Protect yourself by using latex or nitrile gloves during the oil change. Oil is a toxic product that can cause irritation when it comes into contact with your skin.

Do a quick mental review of the steps you need to take to do the oil change. Since many boaters do oil changes only once or twice a year, it's easy to forget an important step:

- Let your engine warm before doing the oil change so the oil is less viscous. But don't warm your engine and then immediately begin pumping out the old oil. Let your engine sit for a while to allow as much oil as possible to drain back into the sump.
- Use a "closed system" to transfer used oil to a receptacle. An electric or manual spill-proof pump or extractor, permanently connected to a valved fitting in the oil sump area of your engine is preferable to a transfer system that you have to put in place each time you do an oil change. A "closed system" also makes the job go more quickly with less chance for spills. If you don't have a fitted oil sump pump, ask your local engine shop about making one for you.
- Lay out oil absorbent pads on the engine room floor underneath the sump fitting, the used oil receptacle and any oil filters that you will also change.
- Use a receptacle strong enough to hold warm engine oil without melting. Plastic is a petroleum by-product and oil can act as a solvent for some kinds of plastic container. Preferably, use a receptacle that has a lid. Keep your empty oil jugs and caps around from one oil change to the next to use as receptacles for used oil.
- Temporarily disable your bilge pump so that it doesn't cycle on in the case of a spill.
- Bag your oil filter. Slip a heavy plastic freezer bag around your oil filter prior to twisting it off. If it's on so tight you need to use a filter wrench, take a few turns with the wrench, then slip on the freezer bag and continue unscrewing the filter with your hands. The plastic bag will catch any oil that drips down the side of the filter.
  - Top off your oil.
  - Immediately mop up any oil spills on the engine, hoses and the floor using an oil-absorbent pad.
  - Make sure to turn your bilge pump back on.
  - Dispose of all used oil, absorbent pads, filters, plastic bags and gloves in an approved oil recycling facility at your marina or somewhere else nearby.

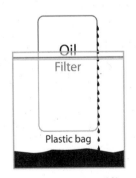

Fig. 22.2: *Bagging an oil filter*

Internet Search Term

"oil change" boat

CHAPTER 24

Boat Green with that Green Liquid in Your Engine

Use antifreeze wisely.
Don't freeze out the marine environment.

That lime-green liquid you pour into your engine should actually be called antifreeze/coolant. Instead, we call it antifreeze for short, but it does much more than prevent the water in your engine's cooling system from freezing during the winter. Your engine's cooling system works to transfer heat away from the engine and maintain the correct engine operating temperature. Circulating coolant water with antifreeze accomplishes this by transferring heat from engine areas where it is generated and carrying this heat to a radiator where it is cooled. A mixture of antifreeze/coolant helps to reduce the risk of the engine not only freezing in winter, but of it overheating as well. Antifreeze/coolant also inhibits rust and corrosion buildup in your engine's cooling system.

But freezing and overheating protection, rust and corrosion prevention come at a price. Ethylene glycol, the principal chemical used in producing antifreeze poses health risks to humans and pets, and can kill marine organisms by lowering levels of oxygen in the water as it biodegrades.

Facts about Antifreeze

Antifreeze is a clear, colorless, sweet-tasting liquid. Green or orange color is added by the manufacturer for identification purposes only. Because of its smell and taste, it is attractive to pets, animals and small children.

Antifreeze Recycling

Antifreeze can be recycled in two main ways:

1. Closed-loop recycling. A filtration system is attached to the coolant system of the engine and the used ethylene glycol is pumped through and filtered.

2. Open-loop recycling. A filtration system is attached to a container of used antifreeze. It is pumped from the container, filtered and placed into the engine's coolant system or into a clean container

If swallowed, however, it causes depression, cardiac and respiratory failure, kidney failure and ultimately brain damage.

Ethylene glycol is the common component of antifreeze. Some antifreeze is made with propylene glycol, a less-toxic cousin of ethylene glycol. At this time, used ethylene glycol is not classified as a hazardous waste by the US Environmental Protection Agency because of its chemical composition, and because it is easily recyclable and reused. Most states have statutory regulations governing the disposal and recycling of used antifreeze.

Antifreeze leaches heavy metals from the solder and engine parts it passes over. These metals are often found in high concentrations in used antifreeze, making in even more harmful to human health and the marine environment. Once shown to have heavy metals in it, antifreeze is considered a hazardous waste.

Silicates are the compounds used in antifreeze to inhibit rust and corrosion. These compounds can also precipitate out, causing damage to pumps, seals and lines. Some engine manufacturers are recommending low-silicate antifreeze.

Steps You Can Take

- Use antifreeze manufactured with propylene glycol rather than ethylene glycol. (Confused about the glycols? Think "PG." Propylene glycol is less toxic.)
- Check with your engine manufacturer or engine repair shop to see if a low-silicate antifreeze will work in your engine.
- Check with your engine manufacturer or engine repair shop about whether you can use recycled antifreeze in your engine; if so, use it.
- Never mix different kinds of antifreezes. Don't mix propylene glycol with ethylene glycol, or a low-silicate antifreeze with a high-silicate blend. Pump out all of your old antifreeze before changing to another.

- Keep used antifreeze in sealed containers away from children, livestock, pets or wild animals.
- Don't pour antifreeze onto the ground.
- Don't pour antifreeze into surrounding waters or into municipal sewer systems.
- Don't mix antifreeze with other engine fluids such as gasoline or diesel fuel. It can't be recycled if it's not pure antifreeze.
- Recycle antifreeze at approved facilities at your marina. If your marina doesn't have antifreeze recycling, call a nearby boatyard and ask if they do. Also, call a local recycling hotline or your state department of environmental protection for information about where to recycle used antifreeze.

Internet Search Terms
antifreeze environment; "propylene glycol"; "ethylene glycol" environment; antifreeze engines boats

CHAPTER 25

Keep Your Engine in Top Shape

A well-maintained engine benefits you and the environment.

M any sections of this book are devoted to the steps you can take to improve engine performance, decrease engine maintenance and benefit the marine environment. Beyond these suggestions and recommendations, there are some basic steps that all boaters should routinely take to make sure their engines, diesel or gas, are in top shape. You may have a mechanic looking after your boat's engine, but your mechanic can't be with you at all times. A complete guide on marine engine maintenance would require its own separate book. However, there are a few essential aspects of engine performance and maintenance that every boater should know and regularly practice. For more specific instruction consult your engine manual or your engine mechanic.

The Four Horsemen of Horsepower

All engines, diesel or gas, need four very basic elements to operate:

1. **Fuel.** Okay, it doesn't get much more basic than this, but all engines need fuel in order to operate, not just fuel in the tanks, but clean fuel delivered to the combustion chamber of the cylinder on time and in the right amount.

Steps You Can Take

- Make certain your fuel supply is clean.
- Periodically have your fuel tanks inspected. Have them cleaned out if needed.

- Trace your fuel lines from the tank to the engine looking for sign of wear, chafing, loose hose clamps or leakage. Repair or replace any problems you find.
- Regularly change your fuel filters. Use the smallest filter size (measured in microns) that will still maintain the fuel flow your engine needs. Your engine manual or mechanic can tell you the correct size.
- Consider installing parallel secondary fuel filters (secondary filtration takes place before primary filtration, which happens directly before fuel is delivered to the fuel injector pump). Parallel fuel filters mean that if one filter clogs the other will be available for service immediately, and you need not stop your boat to change the filter.
- Have your fuel injectors inspected and serviced regularly.
- Be sure that your fuel tank is vented and grounded
- Consider using alternative fuels; see chapters 12 and 13 on biodiesel and ethanol.
- Carry spare fuel filters at all times.

2. **Air.** A mixture of air and fuel is ignited in your engine's cylinders, explosively moving the pistons, the crankshaft, the propeller and, ultimately, your boat. In a gasoline engine, this mixture is regulated by a carburetion device and delivered to the boat's cylinders where it is ignited by a spark. In traditional diesel engines, air is super-heated by compression of the cylinders, and then diesel fuel is sprayed into that super-heated air, causing the explosion that drives the engine.

Steps You Can Take

- If you have an air filter, make sure that it is changed or cleaned regularly.
- If you do not have a closed crankcase ventilation system, consider installing one to prevent blowby gases from contaminating your engine room and the environment. See chapter 22 on crankcase ventilation.
- Make sure your engine room has adequate airflow to it. Don't allow anything to block air ducts or your air filters.
- Carry spare air filters at all times.

3. **Oil.** Since engines have many moving surfaces where metal rubs against metal, oil is needed for lubrication to reduce friction, and the buildup of heat.

Steps You Can Take

- Inspect the length of your oil system from engines to filter to oil cooler, if present. Check for sign of wear, chafing, loose hose clamps or leakage. Repair or replace any problems you find.
- Change your oil regularly, and practice good oil change habits. See chapter 23 on performing an oil change.
- Use the proper oil grade and weight for your engine and the operating conditions you find yourself in.
- Check your oil each time before you start your engine.
- Make sure your oil pressure gauges read accurately and function correctly.
- Have your oil tested periodically for signs of engine problems.
- Carry spare oil filters at all times.

4. **Water.** From the explosion taking place within engines, to the friction of metal moving over metal, engines generate heat that must be dissipated in order to prevent the engine from over-heating and potentially deforming the metal parts. Water, either freshwater or saltwater, is the primary constituent of most marine engine cooling systems.

Steps You Can Take

- Inspect the length of your cooling system from the header intake to the radiator. Check hoses for sign of wear, chafing, loose hose clamps or leakage. Repair or replace any problems you find.
- Change your coolant periodically.
- Use antifreeze that reduces risk to marine environment. See chapter 24 on antifreeze.
- Install an expansion tank in your cooling system to receive coolant overflow so that it doesn't flow into the bilge.
- Check your coolant level each time before you start your engine.
- Inspect your freshwater and raw water pumps and lines for signs of wear and damage.
- Inspect the impellers on your water pumps regularly.
- Carry a spare set of impellers at all times.
- Make sure your engine temperature gauges read accurately and function correctly.

The Most Important Step You Can Take

Get out and use your boat! Engines, particularly diesel engines, present fewer problems when they are used.

Internet Search Terms

"marine engine maintenance"; "diesel engine maintenance"; "gasoline engine maintenance"

CHAPTER 26

Use Solar Power

Mariners have long harnessed the power of the sun.

Since the first human raised a sail, or recognized the propulsive power of tidal currents, mariners have harnessed the power of the sun. Thermally, the sun contributes to the Earth's winds. Gravitationally, the sun along with the moon, create the Earth's tides and tidal currents. As modern humans, we can also harness the sun's power. By using the sun to assist us in propulsion, heating and electricity generation we decrease our reliance on fossil fuels, which benefits the bodies of water we boat on and the bodies of land we inhabit.

In this section, we'll look at harnessing the sun's power for electrical generation and heating. Sailboaters are already taking advantage of the sun's propulsive power. The following discusses the use of solar power.

Harnessing Solar Power

Oil. War. The Middle East. Its sounds like the prelude to a story about fossil fuel, but this all too familiar triangle is intimately related to solar power. In fact, the modern history of solar power can be traced to the desert outside of Cairo and an inventor-entrepreneur named Frank Shuman, from Pennsylvania.

Much like Rudolph Diesel perfecting his non-fossil fuel burning engines during the same years, Frank Shuman had a vision of an industrial age free of reliance on fossil fuels. Building on the successes and failures of previous European and American inventors, Shuman tested and perfected a steam-driven irrigation pump with an engine run by solar-heated water in the fields outside his home in Tacony, Pennsylvania. Then, realizing it would never compete with coal-generated systems, Shuman moved his operation to the desert outside of Cairo, Egypt, where he constructed an even better solar-driven motor, complete with sophisticated collectors and a storage system for retaining the hot water that powered his pumps. Shuman's system was a resounding success, and his Sun Power Company appeared destined for a bright future, until World War I began. Egypt was engulfed in the conflict. Shuman's plant was destroyed. He died before the Armistice was signed. By the War's end, oil had been discovered under the Middle East deserts, and resurrecting a renewable energy source was all but forgotten for the next 60 years.

While Shuman used the sun as a source of thermal energy to drive machines, he pioneered the basic elements of solar electric energy still used today: a collector system, a storage system and good access to the sun.

The photovoltaic effect, which converts sunlight into electrical energy, was discovered in 1839 by the French physicist, A. E. Becquerel. One hundred years later, Bell Labs scientist Russell Ohl discovered the photovoltaic properties of silicon and created the first photovoltaic cell.

The development of solar electrical generation has closely followed the rise and ebb of petroleum prices. A rise in oil prices in the 1970s stimulated research and development into solar electricity. As oil prices fell, and government tax incentives for solar research disappeared, solar energy research declined. But research and interest in solar energy is on the rise again, with the realization that world oil reserves are reaching their limit, and even greater interest in energy generation that does not produce greenhouse gases or contribute to global warming.

Onboard Solar Systems

Initially, recreational boaters looked to solar energy as a means of trickle-charging batteries and reducing the load of energy-hungry electronics and other appliances. But new developments in solar technologies, like diesel-solar-electric hybrid systems capable of powering boats under solar power alone (see chapter 15) mean that solar energy has a promising future for boaters.

The basic features of an onboard solar system are the same today as they were in Frank Shuman's time: collectors (in our case photovoltaic cells), storage (usually lead-acid batteries) and some means of regulating or controlling the energy produced by the PV cells (most often a charge controller).

The most important aspect of designing a solar system for your boat is determining the demand you place on your electrical system. Your electrical demand is the number of amp-hours per day you require to run the equipment aboard your boat. GPS, radar, radios, computers, chart plotters, stereos, microwaves, toasters, blenders, refrigerators, hair dryers, lighting, fans and the host of other equipment and appliances draw energy from the batteries aboard your boat. That energy needs to be replaced, and it is typically replaced in several ways:

- When running your engine, the alternator produces electricity that recharges your batteries.
- When not running your main engine, you may run your generator (another engine) to produce electricity.
- When not running any of your engines, if you're at a dock with a shore power connection, you plug into the land-based power grid and use electrical current from the grid to directly run appliances or to feed an inverter and charger that converts the alternating current from the grid into direct current that can either run appliances or charge your battery.

All of these methods of energy generation have one thing in common: they rely on fossil fuels, although the power grid may derive a small percentage of power from renewal sources such as solar or wind power.

A solar energy system, on the other hand, uses a photovoltaic cell to produce the electricity that replaces the energy you withdrew from your batteries when running your devices and appliances. When running a generator or plugging into shore power, we don't think very much about how much energy we need to replace. We simply run the generator long enough or stay connected to shore power until our batteries are charged. But solar cells supply only a certain amount of energy that, depending upon the size and number of the PV cells, may or may not be enough to replace the energy you typically withdraw. That is why you must size your solar system to the energy demands of your boat, or if that is not possible, use your solar system as an adjunct to the other methods of generating energy.

The Benefits of Onboard Solar Energy

- Clean, renewable energy generation. No pollutants. No discharge of gases.
- Reduced fossil fuel emissions from engines into the water, lessening the impact of boat operation on the marine environment.
- Solar panels come with 20-25 year warranties.
- Zero maintenance of PV cells, other than wiping the surface clean.
- Other elements of the system like batteries need normal maintenance.
- Increased safety by reducing the need to burn fossil fuels.
- Potentially decreased operating costs of the vessel by requiring less fuel for generators. There is an initial investment in the purchase and installation of the solar system. Depending upon amount of use, the investment may be returned in as little as two to three years.
- Decreased demand on local power grids when connected to shore power.
- Increased time available to be at anchor without running a generator, thus reducing noise levels and enhancing enjoyment.

The principal drawback of solar energy is that it requires sunlight, which varies in terms of hours and radiation depending upon the time of year and geographical location.

Steps You Can Take

Want to install a solar system on your boat? Consider these steps:

- Use a solar power load calculator to determine the size of the solar system you will need to meet the energy demands of your boat's operation. Remember that you will still receive many benefits of using solar energy even if you cannot install a system that meets 100% of your energy demands. See Internet Search Terms in this chapter to find a multitude of solar power load calculators online.
- Install a charge controller that regulates the electrical output of your solar cells as they feed into your batteries and electrical system.
- Size your battery system to meet the capacity of your solar cells. You may need to install additional batteries to handle the capacity of the solar cells you install.
- Choose a location for your solar panels that is out of the way of important equipment on your boat and receives the most amount of

sunlight. The roof of cabins and atop davits are two such popular places. Other mounts can be found for rails, but these panels will need to be continually adjusted to receive the most direct sunlight. If you're building your own boat, consider having recesses for PV cells built into the superstructure.

- Consider installing a battery desulfator along with your solar system. See chapter 29 for additional information on the role of battery desulfators in prolonging the life and charging capacity of lead-acid batteries.
- Connect your solar system through a relay to your anchor light. Now, when the sun goes down, the anchor light comes on. When the sun rises, the anchor light goes off, much like the solar-powered walkway lights available for home use.
- See Figure 26.1, Photovoltaic system with automatic anchor light, for a diagram of the solar system in use on the author's boat.

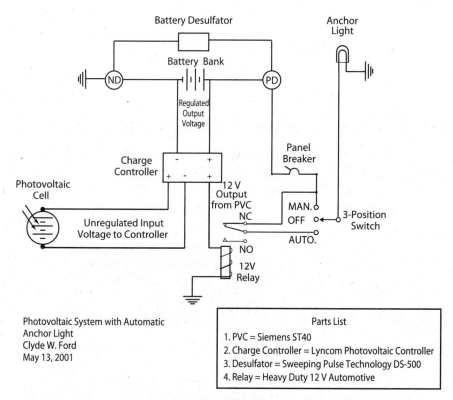

Fig. 26.1: *Photovoltaic system with automatic anchor light*

Not All Solar Cells Are Created Equal

Different kinds of solar cells behave differently. Some may be more appropriate than others for your onboard solar installation. Most commercially available solar panels are made from silicon, but there are three basic types of solar cells, classified according to their manufacturing process and operating characteristics.

Solar Hot Water on Boats

Most boats obtain hot water from one of two sources: water heated from a running engine, or water heated in a diesel, propane or electric hot water tank. Most often, hot water is obtained from a combination of these two sources. At anchor, or at dock, boaters will run a generator, or a diesel or propane furnace, to heat water.

The sun offers another alternative for hot water aboard a boat. Many boaters already use "Solar Shower" bags for heating the water that they use to bathe. The bags, lined with black plastic on one side and a transparent plastic on the other, are filled with water and then placed under sunlight, which enters through the transparent side, strikes the black

Comparison of Solar Cell Technologies

SOLAR CELL TECHNOLOGY	BENEFITS AND DRAWBACKS
Single-crystal silicon or mono-crystalline	Highly reliable. Expensive to produce. Usually available in rigid frames of rounded photovoltaic cells.
Multi-crystal silicon or poly-crystalline	Less expensive to produce. Quality varies according to the purity of the silicon used.
Thin-film voltaics, two types:	
Amorphous silicon	Very cost effective. No inherent crystalline structure. Look like glass. Can be deposited on surfaces like plastics, metals and fabrics making them adaptable and portable. Less efficient than mono- or poly- crystalline cells but capable of responding to wider spectrum of light than a mono-crystalline cell and thereby producing electricity in low-light conditions at dusk and dawn.
Copper Indium Gallium Selenide or CIGS	Relatively newer thin film technology. More efficient that amorphous silicon yet still as adaptable.

Fig. 26.2

side and heats the water. Don't kid yourself, this simple piece of equipment can produce scalding hot water even when the outside air temperature is cool. All other methods of solar hot water heating aboard a boat are variations on this basic idea (see Figure 26.3). Cold water is run through a solar collector where the sun's energy heats it. In modern solar collectors, water is often sandwiched between a glazed top layer and a bottom black layer of material. The glazed surface allows sunlight to heat the water but does not allow thermal radiation to escape. Between the two layers, water may be forced through piping for more efficient heating or collected in a tank.

Hot water from a solar heating system can be fed back into a boat's hot water collection tank, fed through baseboard radiator pipes for cabin heat or used directly for hot water from faucets, if the system has its own built-in collection tank. Solar collectors in a variety of sizes can be mounted on exposed surfaces of a boat and linked together in series for more heating capacity.

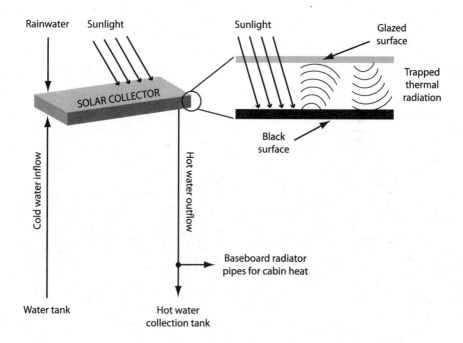

Fig. 26.3: *An onboard solar heating system.*

Solar Cabin Heat

Air can be heated as easily as water. Imagine that in Figure 26.3, cold air is being forced through a solar collector then into air ducts that lead to the interior spaces of a boat. This is a forced air solar heating system, and solar collectors with 12 volt fans are manufactured to provide such solar heating systems.

Benefits and Drawbacks of Solar Heating Systems

Solar heating systems are easy to construct, have few mechanical parts to maintain or wear out and produce zero emissions or waste. There is minimal, if any cost, for fuel, operations or maintenance.

One drawback is that their efficiency depends upon the amount of sunlight available. These systems may not be sufficient in colder climates. Back-up heat sources may be needed.

Another Form of Solar Heating

High-density polyethylene (HDPE) allows filtered sunlight into your boat's cabin, but the material absorbs sunlight and converts it to heat, in effect, acting as a thermal radiator to raise inside temperature. Enough light is still allowed through the drapes, providing a muted view outside. HDPE drape material is often fitted with small suction cups to make installation easy.

Solar Cooling

Both active and passive solar cooling solutions exist for recreational vessels operating in climates where air-conditioning is the norm. Solar-operated ventilation fans circulate air. Low solar-gain windows, ports, overhead skylights and hatches manufactured with a barrier layer or treated with barrier film reduce the load on air-conditioning systems.

Internet Search Terms

"solar energy"; "photovoltaic cells"; "solar energy" boating; "solar power load calculator"; "solar heating", "solar hot water", "solar hot water" boats, "solar heating" boats, "HDPE drapes", "barrier film" "solar cooling", "solar fans", "solar skylights", "solar hatches"

CHAPTER 27

Running with the Wind

Wind power can provide for a range of onboard needs.

W ind power has long propelled boats. Sailing is the art and science of harnessing the power of the wind. And since the wind is essentially produced through differential heating of land and water masses, wind power is really the result of solar power. But beyond using it to propel a boat, we can also use the wind to drive the blades of a turbine that generates electricity. Both sailboats and powerboats can harness the power of the wind.

Benefits of Wind Power

Like solar power, wind power is a clean form of generating electricity with no harmful by-products released into the environment; no greenhouse gases are produced by wind generation. It reduces both the need to connect to shore power and the need to run fuel-based generators to produce electricity. Wind power increases battery life and can be used in areas even when there is no sun.

Considerations for Wind Power

Wind turbines for boats range in size from units that produce a watt or less to those capable of producing 500 watts. The smaller ones are best suited for trickle-charging batteries; the larger can form the central part of a green power system. Noise, size, weight, cost, location and intended use are the major factors to take into account when considering wind power.

Steps You Can Take

- Size the wind generator appropriately for the application you are intending.

- Make sure you have a charge controller either built-in to the wind generator or installed inline so your batteries are protected from overcharging and can receive the proper amount of charge.

- Consider the noise of the generator. Before purchasing, listen to several units operating on other boats. Not all wind generators produce the same amount of noise. You don't want a wind generator disturbing your peace at anchor, or the peace of other boaters around you.

- Make sure you are able to mount the unit high enough and out of the way of the crew, lines and other equipment.

- Make sure the weight of the unit does not compromise the stability of your boat (especially for heavier units).

- Make sure the torque of the blades when the unit is operating in a stiff breeze does not compromise the stability or controllability of your boat (heavier units).

- If you intend to integrate wind, solar and fuel generators, be certain you have a charge controller capable of handling energy generation from different sources.

- Wind power can make sense even for power boats. While running under power, most boats will use their alternators to charge battery banks and run electrical equipment. Some diesel engines, for example, are equipped with alternators that directly produce AC current when the engine is running, enabling them to power equipment while underway. At dock or at anchorage, wind power can be used to keep batteries topped off, or to offset the energy expenditure of appliances and devices. Of course, no boater should intentionally anchor in a high-wind area just to make use of a wind generator, but many units are designed to operate very efficiently in winds of 10 to 15 knots, which are very moderate winds to anchor in.

- Sailboats can also consider a towed generator that uses the force of the water to drive turbines, which produce electricity. Some manufacturers make hybrid units that operate both a water generator and wind generators. One problem reported for towed units: When trailing behind a boat, they have been eaten by sharks!

Resource

"Wind Generator Test." *Sailing Today*, August 2002. This test compared the features and operation of six different wind generators on the market as of 2002.

Internet Search Terms

"wind generator" boat; "wind power" boat; "wind power"; "towed generator" boat

CHAPTER 28

On Dock, Off Grid

Many boats spend most of their time connected to the power grid.

W hether hopping from marina to marina or in its slip at your home port, many boats spend a majority of their time at a dock connected to shore power. Shore power affords us the amenities that we're accustomed to at home, amenities that boaters without generators or large inverters don't have underway such as hot showers, hot water to wash clothes and dishes, microwave ovens, air conditioning — well the list goes on and on. But when connected to shore power, it's easy to forget that our boat is not a small home. While the financial burden of shore power is often insignificant, the environmental impact is not. Boaters can contribute to the health of our global environment by economizing the use of shore power, without sacrificing the amenities it provides. The simplest way to do this is by applying all of the energy-saving principles you use at home to your boat when it's connected to the power grid.

No Free Lunch

When it comes to power consumption, there is no free lunch, even on a boat. Whether you're running appliances and devices off batteries, off shore power or off electricity produced by a generator, most of the time you are expending energy or causing a power plant somewhere to expend energy to produce the electricity that you need. These energy expenditures impact the environment, some more so than others. Wise energy use aboard your vessel will reduce overall operating costs, decrease maintenance and protect the health of the environment on the water and the land.

Steps You Can Take

- If keeping your batteries topped off through your inverter is the only reason you're leaving your boat connected to shore power, consider other options, such as installing a small solar cell or plugging into shore power only long enough to top off your batteries, then unplugging until they need to be charged again.
- If you periodically run your diesel engine during winter months when you're not cruising (a good practice to keep the engine performing optimally), use that time to recharge your batteries, eliminating the need to plug into shore power.
- If you're using a light bulb to warm the inside of your boat during cold winter months, consider switching to a small space heater with a timer or thermostat. Light bulbs place a large demand on the power grid and, therefore, on the generation of electricity.
- If you're heating the boat from shore power while you're aboard, lower the thermostat seven to ten degrees at night while you're sleeping.
- If you have onboard laundry facilities that you use while on shore power, switch to cold when doing your laundry; 85 – 90% of the energy used to wash your clothes is used to heat the water. By turning the dial to cold on your washing machine, you help the environment, save energy and save money. If you're cruising while washing, also switch to cold. That way you'll lessen the demand on your generator and your fuel supply to heat wash water. Wash full loads of clothes.
- Boats can be notoriously leaky structures where air funnels through gaps in doors or poorly insulated bulkheads. Weatherstrip doors. Add insulation where you can. This will help with both heating and cooling.
- Install low-flow shower heads and faucets.
- Install on-demand faucets. These faucets, available from most marine supply stores, have a small arm that protrudes down from the faucet head. Slight pressure with your hand causes water to flow. Removing that pressure causes the water to stop.

- Switch to LED inside lighting. They are more expensive, but their higher price pays for itself with decreased power demands, which means greater battery life and less time burning fuel running a generator to charge batteries or run the lights.
- Insulate your refrigerator well to reduce thermal loss and power consumption. Consisder installing a fan near your refrigerator's heat exchanger to decrease heat buildup and increase the unit's efficiency.
- Consider alternate sources of power generation such as biofuels, solar and wind power. See sections of this book devoted to these steps you can take.

Internet Search Terms

"energy efficient home"; "power saving tips"

CHAPTER 29

Keep Your Batteries Going ...
and Going ... and Going

Keep lead-acid batteries an environmental success story.

L ead-acid batteries can be classified as an environmental success
story. More than 97% of all battery lead is recycled, compared
with 26% of tires and glass bottles, 45% of newspapers and 55% of
aluminum soft drink cans. One reason that lead-acid batteries are recycling winners is their closed-loop life cycle. Used batteries are sent to
registered recyclers who reclaim the 60-80% of the lead and the plastic before sending it on to new battery manufacturers who reuse these

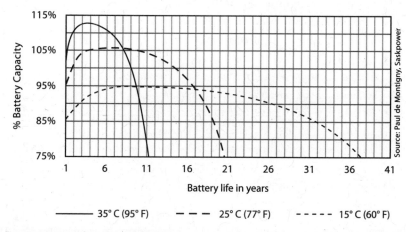

Fig. 29.1: *Battery life versus temperature*

elements. The lead and the plastic in your boat have been — and will be — reused many times. It goes without saying, then, that we should keep up this high success rate by always returning our old batteries when we purchase new ones.

But the battery story doesn't end here. While recycling our marine batteries keeps them out of landfills, and out of our waters, keeping our batteries supplying power for as long as possible is also important. Longer, healthier battery life means less expense and less reliance on fossil fuel for the electrical demands aboard our vessels.

There are no secrets to extending the life of your batteries, but there are some basic principles and steps that you can follow. Regardless of the kind of lead-acid battery that you have (wet, gel or glass mat), here are some steps you can take toward longer battery life.

Steps You Can Take

- Size your batteries properly for the electrical loads aboard your boat. An undersized battery system will result in shorter battery life. See information on boat load calculator below.
- Keep your batteries in a cool place. Temperature has a huge effect on battery life. Higher temperature accelerates the chemical reactions going on inside a lead-acid battery, shortening its usable life. In closed-cell batteries, increased temperature can also cause increased pressure inside the battery cells, further accelerating the chemical reactions. See Figure 29.1.
- Very cold weather can adversely affect batteries as well. Deeply discharged batteries can freeze solid in extremely cold weather.
- Keep your wet-cell batteries topped off with water. Battery plates exposed to air will begin to form sulfate crystals, reducing the charge capacity of the battery.
- Don't let your batteries sit in an uncharged state without any energy entering them. Recharge your batteries immediately after use.
- Use solar or wind power to trickle-charge your batteries. See chapters 26 and 27 on solar and wind power generation.
- Use the appropriate charging stages and voltage levels for the type of battery in your vessel.
- Don't mix and match battery types. Wet cells have different charging needs from gel cells or glass mat batteries.

- Find and eliminate unnecessary sources of parasitic drain on your battery that are drawing energy even when your ignition key is switched off.
- Regularly inspect your batteries.
- Use distilled water, not tap water, when filling wet-cell batteries. Tap water may have minerals and impurities that will contaminate a battery's electrolyte solution.
- Sulfation, the buildup of lead sulfate on battery plates, hardens them and prevents batteries from holding a charge. All lead-acid batteries go through sulfation. This is the battery aging process. Install a battery desulfator, a device that pulses your batteries at a frequency that lessens and even reverses sulfation. See Internet search terms below.
- Always practice safety around batteries: wear rubber gloves and safety goggles, remove jewelry and be very careful of metal tools around batteries (insulate wrenches with electric tape).

Internet Search Terms
batteries recycling; "extending battery life"; "battery desulfators"

CHaPTeR 30

Best Boatyard Practices

Boatyards are partners in protecting our waters.

E very boat, and every boater, spends time in a boatyard. It's part of the ritual of boating. Our vessels go "on the hard" for inspections, repairs, routine maintenance and modifications. Boatyards are also important stakeholders in protecting the marine environment. They are faced with handling the residue from the maintenance and repair of our vessels; residue that is often toxic and damaging to the marine environment and to the health of boatyard workers and customers. Most boatyards have environmental guidelines that govern the practices of their workers and their customers who work on boats. Learning about these guidelines and following them will help boaters partner with boatyards to be good stewards of the marine environment. Before getting work done on your boat, ask the boatyard, "What are your environmental guidelines and standards?"

Many of the best management practices for boatyards are also best management practices for boaters working on their boats at any time and in any place. Some of these are discussed later in more depth. Still, it's important for boaters to have an overview of the general standards that should be in place at a boatyard. If you're faced with choosing between yards to work on your boat, their environmental standards may be a deciding factor. Here are some steps you can take to work with the boatyard to protect the surrounding waters.

Steps You Can Take

• Ask the yard for a handout, a written description, or take notes on

137

the environmental practices in place at the yard. Follow these practices as you work on your boat.

- If you have any questions about working on your boat, ask the yard if what you intend to do is in compliance with environmental standards.
- Ask the yard to describe for you how hazardous waste is handled and where hazardous waste is to be stored — used oil drums, bilge water drums, gasoline drums, rags saturated with solvent.[1]

Hull Preparation

Use a dustless or vacuum sander (see chapter 35) to prepare your hull for painting indoors, if possible over a hard, non-porous surface. If working outdoors without a vacuum sander, or where your activities produce uncontrolled dust and chips, tent the boat. Placing a sheet of heavy plastic under the boat will provide a non-porous surface that's easily cleaned up and prevents particulate matter from escaping to ground and finding its way into the water. Clean up immediately after hull preparation, especially before any predicted rainfall if you're working outside. Store spent dust, scrapings and other debris in a covered container. The yard should have in place methods of disposing of such waste material.

Hull Painting

Using bottom paints that are the least damaging to the marine environment (see chapter 32 on bottom painting), paint your hull indoors if possible, over a non-porous surface. If painting outside, lay down a tarp weighted at the edges, or paint over a hard, non-porous surface that is easily cleaned up.

Spray painting ideally should be done indoors in a well-ventilated area over a non-porous surface. If spraying outdoors, the area to be painted should be tented over a non-porous tarp or covering to prevent overspray from entering the atmosphere or reaching the ground and migrating into nearby waters. Outdoor tents should be well-ventilated.

Cleaning paint brushes, rollers or guns can generate large amounts of hazardous or special wastes. Minimize waste production by using separate cans of cleaner that are graduated in purity and reusing the cleaner in successive steps. By letting the cleaning solvent settle and decanting off the clean solvent, you can reuse the solvent indefinitely.

Engine Maintenance

Engine maintenance and repairs should be done in a dedicated work area over a non-porous surface with no floor drain. The area must be kept dry and not "washed out" into the yard during cleaning. Waste oils, fuel and antifreeze then can be collected for proper disposal.

Limit engine work performed in the water to routine engine maintenance: tune-ups, oil changes and minor repairs. Engine replacement or removal must be monitored carefully to prevent discharge of engine fluids into the water. The bilge should be dry before service is begun and the bilge pump turned off. Oil-absorbent pads should be used to catch spills. The bilge should be inspected and cleaned before the bilge pump is used again.

Internet Search Terms

"best management practices" boatyards

CHAPTER 31

Bilge Busting

Prevent pollution with diverter valves,
bilge socks and bacteria.

A bilge may be one of the most environmentally unfriendly places on a boat. Wastewater builds up in the bilge, along with whatever else finds its way down to this low spot. Bilges are primarily meant to catch seawater that infiltrates into a boat and periodically pump it out. But other fluids, like oil and coolant laced with antifreeze, often find their way into the bilge, and so there's a risk of pumping them overboard as well. It's illegal to pump contaminated bilge water overboard. But more importantly, it's unnecessary. Even if your bilge water is contaminated with oil, there are steps you can take to clean it up before pumping it overboard.

Install a Diverter Valve

All boats should come with a Y-diverter valve installed on at least one line running from the bilge. Similar to the diverter valves installed on holding tanks, this would allow for the contaminated bilge water to be pumped directly into a container. The setup is very straightforward, as shown in Figure 31.1.

Bilge filled with oily water? Turn the diverter valve one way and pump into a container that you empty at an oil recycling station. Bilge clean? Leave the diverter valve open so the bilge pumps overboard.

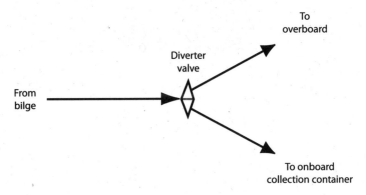

Fig. 31.1: *Basic diagram of bilge with diverter valve.*

Use the Right Bilge Sock

Most boaters are familiar with bilge socks, sacks filled with material that absorbs oil but not water. But did you know that not all bilge socks are created equal? Their effectiveness is measured by four characteristics:

- Initial absorption — how quickly the oil-absorbent material absorbs oil.
- Overall absorption — how much total oil is absorbed.
- Swelling — how much the bilge sock swells. This is very important for tight spaces, like the bilge. Have you ever had a sock swell so much that it's hard to get out, and you have to wring out some oil to remove it? That kind of defeats the purpose of the sock.
- Retention — a measure of how much of the absorbed oil stays within the bilge sock once you lift it from the bilge to dispose of it.

Bilge socks are also made of different oil-absorbent materials. A 2000 study conducted in Buzzards Bay, Massachusetts,[1] tested various types of bilge socks based on the above four criteria. The results show clear winners and losers in the battle of the bilge. Polymer bilge socks outperform the competition. Read the label the next time you buy a bilge sock. Ask your chandlery to carry polymer bilge socks, or order from the resource section below. By the way, the bilge socks and pads with oil-eating bacteria are the ones that performed the worst in this test, but they are frequently advertised as the most environmentally friendly.

Comparison test of bilge socks

TYPE OF MATERIAL	INITIAL ABSORPTION	OVERALL ABSORPTION	SWELLING	RETENTION
Polypropylene	Medium to High	Good	Low	Poor
Biological	Fails	Fails	Fails	Fails
Foam	High	Poor	High	Poor
Polymer*	High	Good	Low	Good
Cellulose	High	Good	Low	Poor
Polypropylene	Medium to High	Good	Low	Poor
Biological	Fails most tests	Fails	Fails	Fails

Fig. 31.2: * denotes the best bilge sock to use

Bugs in the Bilge

Bugs may not work in bilge socks, but they do work directly in your bilge. You've probably heard of oil-eating bacteria dispersed over a major oil spill to help with the cleanup. This process is known as bioremediation, and it's now available to the average boater. It's easy to grow a colony of oil-eating bugs in your bilge, and it's good for your bilge and for the water.

Oil-eating bacteria are available from your chandlery or online in large dry tablets or in a powder that you mix with water and then pour into the bilge. Initially, you want to treat the system at least twice in a two-week period; then as long as there's liquid around with oil in it, the bacteria will be happy and grow. After digesting the oil, these bacteria turn it into a harmless substance. In many cases, oily bilge water will be fit to pump overboard after the bacteria have been left for several weeks.

Other Steps You Can Take

- If your engine isn't fitted with an oil drip pan underneath it, construct one from a deep-dish aluminum baking tray lined with oil-absorbent pads.
- Once you remove a bilge pad, allow it to dry before disposing of it in the recycling area of your marina.
- Check your engine regularly for leaks and correct the source of any leaks. Placing clean oil-absorbent pads under your engine will alert you to the presence and location of any leaks.

- If your coolant overflow drains directly into your bilge, install a coolant expansion tank to collect coolant and recycle it into your coolant system.

Resource

Lakefront Enterprises. Makers of polymer bilge sock tested and approved for use by a variety of local, state, federal agencies. Read bilge sock study on their website: www.enviro-bond.com. Buy polymer bilge socks directly from them.

Internet Search Terms

"polymer bilge socks"; "bioremediation recreational boats"; "oil-eating bacteria" recreational boats

CHAPTER 32

Bottoms Up

Choose the right bottom paint and protect the marine environment.

Wh

hen your boat is in the water, the bottom of the hull is a part of the marine ecosystem — the marine environment affects the hull, and the hull affects the marine environment. And both can affect each other harshly. If left untreated barnacles, algae and other aquatic organisms on the hull not only interfere with the performance, but they can actually damage the surfaces they attach to. On the other hand, the chemicals used to prevent their attachment and growth have traditionally been some of the most toxic and harmful to the marine environment. Their job is to kill marine life. Unfortunately, they do their job so well that they affect marine life well beyond the organisms that attack the hull. While many of the most harmful products applied to boat bottoms have been curtailed in recent years, it takes some preparation to reach a good compromise between protecting the hull from the marine environment and protecting the marine environment from the hull.

For many years, Tributyltin (TBT) was the active compound in bottom paint used to prevent the attachment and growth of marine organisms. But recent studies have shown that the leeching of TBT from hulls has disastrous and irreversible effects on marine organisms. Severe shellfish deformities, reduced growth of algae and toxic effects on young fish have all been traced to TBT.[1] The deaths of sea otters and bottlenose dolphins have also been linked with the compound.[2]

One of the saddest recent findings is that, as TBT works its way up the food chain, its presence in the bodies of orcas and dolphin affects their ability to hear and to echolocate, which may explain an increased incidence of beaching by these marine mammals.[3]

TBT is an endocrine-disrupting chemical (EDC) whose effect does not stop at the water's edge. Elevated levels of TBT are also found in human beings, a reminder that what we place on the bottom of our boat can affect our health and well-being as well. The United States Environmental Protection Agency (EPA) issued a limited ban on TBT bottom paints in 1988; the International Marine Organization (IMO) issued a similar ban in 2001. TBT is still used as a bottom coat on aluminum boats.

In response to the ban on TBT, copper rather than tin was introduced as a biocide in bottom paints. Actually, copper has been around as an anti-fouling agent since the early tall ships days when copper sheets were nailed to the sides of vessels to prevent barnacle growth. But while copper is a naturally occurring element in the environment, its increased concentration has exceeded EPA levels in a number of crowded ports and marinas around the country. Some manufacturers have introduced new compounds for more slowly releasing copper. Other active agents such as the herbicides iragol and diuron also have been introduced into bottom paints. Still, the environmental challenge is that these agents persist and build to toxic levels that affect organisms throughout the food chain.

With TBT banned and copper-based bottom paints in question, what's an environmentally conscious boater to do? The US Coast Guard has turned to an innovative bottom paint, developed in response to the original ban on TBT in the late-1980s. It contains a catalyst that reacts with oxygen in the water and sunlight to produce a continual low level of hydrogen peroxide, a substance that prevents barnacles, mollusks and tubeworms from attaching to hulls. After its release, the hydrogen peroxide harmlessly decomposes back into water and oxygen. All US Coast Guard vessels are now being bottom-painted with this product from the US company ePaint. After working out production problems with its first product line, ePaint is now available for recreational boaters (see Resources below). One of its nice features is that it can be applied to hulls constructed of any material, including aluminum.

No doubt other similar products will eventually find their way to the marine market.

The right choice of bottom paint is one step toward protecting the marine environment. How you actually remove and apply bottom paint is another. Here are some guidelines you can follow for bottom-painting your boat.

Steps You Can Take

- Choose a new non-metallic, non-toxic bottom paint like ePaint.
- Use dustless or vacuum sanders to remove paint and retain the sanding material.
- Use alternative abrasive materials such as baking soda or corn husks.
- Place tarps or filter cloth under the vessel to collect paint and scraping chips.
- Tent your boat or remove paint in an enclosed structure to contain airborne debris and dust.
- Avoid paint removal activities on windy days if an enclosed maintenance shelter is not available.
- Use minimal abrasion when cleaning antifouling paints.
- Collect all resulting trash, debris, paint chips, fiberglass, blast grit and residue from paint removal. Dispose of properly.
- Paint residue and blast grit must not be disposed of in the trash or construction materials dumpsters, unless tested by an approved laboratory and certified as not being lead based.
- Avoid in-water bottom cleaning, hull scraping or any other process occurring in the water that could remove antifouling paint and introduce it into the water.
- Take a tip from the old-timers. Add a half-cup of cayenne pepper to a gallon of antifouling paint.

Resources
ePaint pioneered the creation of non-toxic bottom paints that use a steady release of low-level hydrogen peroxide: www.epaint.net
"Antifouling Paint in Fragile Ocean." *Professional Boat Builder* , 105, February/March 2007.

Internet Search Terms
TBT; "anti-fouling copper"; "anti-fouling" "hydrogen peroxide"

CHAPTER 33

Recipes for a Clean Boat

Use environmentally friendly cleaning products.

W̶e boaters spend a lot of time and money keeping our boats clean. We'll often consult with other boaters about what products they use to shine stainless steel, polish brass or oil wood. Many manufacturers of boat cleansing items have gone "green," producing products with a reduced impact on the environment. And that's great. But you might be surprised to know that some of the best cleansing products for your boat are as close as your kitchen cabinet. They're extremely low-cost and offer significant benefits to our environment.

Biodegradable — What Does That Really Mean?

Most products — man-made or natural — are biodegradable, meaning that ultimately they break down and return to nature. The trick is how long that process will take. Uranium-238 will ultimately degrade into a stable, non-radioactive form of lead. The problem is that this takes 4.5 billion years, and along the way, each successive product of the degradation process is radioactive and potentially harmful. A banana peel, on the other hand, degrades in 2-10 days. See Figure 33.1.

The US Federal Trade Commission (FTC) has voluntary guidelines for manufacturers to follow when labeling their products "biodegradable," "recyclable" or any other term to denote a reduced impact on the environment. But these are guidelines only, and the FTC does not have the power or authority to enforce them.

For example, these FTC guidelines say that "biogradable" should mean that a product or its packaging degrades and returns to nature in a "reasonable period of time," given the location it is normally disposed in — landfill, incineration, sewage treatment, etc. That, obviously, leaves a good deal of wiggle room.

Deceptive Product Claims and the Environment

- **Biodegradable.** A trash bag is marketed as "degradable," with no qualification or other disclosure. The marketer relies on soil burial tests to show that the product will decompose in the presence of water and oxygen. The trash bags are customarily disposed of in incineration facilities or at sanitary landfills that are managed in a way that inhibits degradation by minimizing moisture and oxygen. Degradation will be irrelevant for those trash bags that are incinerated, and for those sent to landfills, the marketer does not possess adequate substantiation that the bags will degrade in a reasonably short period of time there. The claim is therefore deceptive.
- **Compostable.** A manufacturer makes an unqualified claim that its package is compostable. Although municipal or institutional composting facilities exist where the product is sold, the package will not break down into usable compost in a home compost pile or device.
- **Recyclable.** A nationally marketed 8 oz. plastic cottage-cheese container displays the Society of the Plastics Industry (SPI) code (which consists of a design of arrows in a triangular shape containing a number and abbreviation identifying the component plastic resin) on the front label of the container, in close proximity to the product name and logo. The manufacturer's conspicuous use of the SPI code in this manner constitutes a recyclability claim. But recycling facilities for this container are available to only a small number of consumers or communities.
- **Ozone safe. Ozone friendly.** An aerosol air freshener is labeled "ozone friendly." Some of the product's ingredients are volatile organic compounds (VOCs) that may cause smog by contributing to ground-level ozone formation. The claim is likely to convey to consumers that the product is safe for the atmosphere as a whole, and is therefore deceptive.[1]

A hazardous product is one which can harm the user or the environment. A substance is considered hazardous if it is toxic (poisonous),

Biodegradable time for common items

ITEM	TIME TO DEGRADE
Cotton rags	1-5 months
Paper	2-5 months
Rope	3-14 months
Orange peels	6 months
Wool socks	1-5 years
Cigarette filters	1-12 years
Tetrapaks (plastics composite) milk cartons	5 years
Leather shoes	25-40 years
Nylon fabric	30-40 years
Plastic bags	10-20 years
Plastic 6-pack holder rings	450 years
Styrofoam cup	1-100 years
Banana peel	2-10 days

Fig. 33.1

flammable, caustic (causes bumps) or chemically reactive. DANGER on a labels means the product is highly toxic; WARNING signals moderate toxicity; CAUTION even less toxicity.

Steps You Can Take

- Read the labels on all products you use on your boat, realizing that manufacturers are not always required to list every ingredient in a product.
- Choose CAUTION labels or better still, look for one with no warnings.
- Remember that labels don't address environmental hazards. Avoid phosphates, chlorinated compounds, petroleum distillates, phenols and formaldehyde. Biodegradable does not mean non-toxic!
- Look for terms like "certified biodegradable" as opposed to "biodegradable," which suggests the presence of an independent standards agency behind the label.
- Use alternative products to clean your boat. See Figure 33.2.

Internet Search Terms

biodegradable; certified biodegradable; half-life; environmental claims; alternative cleaning recipes

Household products you can use

PRODUCT	ALTERNATIVE
Bleach & Borax	Hydrogen peroxide
Detergent & Soap	Elbow grease
Scouring Powders	Baking soda
General Purpose Cleaner	Bicarbonate of soda and vinegar or lemon juice combined with borax paste
Floor Cleaner	One cup white vinegar in 2 gal. water
Window Cleaner	One cup vinegar + 1 qt. warm water. Rinse and squeegee.
Aluminum Cleaner	2 tablespoons of cream of tartar + 1 qt. of hot water
Brass Cleaner	Worcestershire sauce or paste made of equal amounts of salt, vinegar and water. Pour on ketchup. Let it sit, then polish.
Stainless Steel	Clean and polish with a baking soda/water paste
Copper Cleaner	Lemon juice and water
Chrome Cleaner/Polish	Apple cider vinegar to clean; baby oil polish
Fiberglass Stain Remover	Baking soda paste
Mildew Remover	Paste with equal amounts of lemon juice and salt or vinegar and salt. Scrub mildew spots with borax/water solution (½ C. borax to 1 gallon water) using a nylon scouring pad. To prevent mold or mildew from forming, don't rinse off the borax.
Drain Opener	Disassemble or use plumbers snake; toxic substances should not be used in a thru-hull drain
Wood Polish	Olive or almond oil (interior wood only)
Outside Teak	Let it go natural as boaters did for hundreds of years. Wash it down with salt water.
Hand Cleaner	Baby oil or margarine
Air Freshener	Pour vanilla extract on a cotton ball in a saucer. Set out a dish of vinegar, or boil 1 tablespoon white vinegar in 1 cup of water to eliminate cooking odors. Use baking soda in refrigerators, closets and other enclosed areas to absorb odors.

Fig. 33.2

CHAPTER 34

Skirt Your Boat

When sanding or varnishing at the dock, put a skirt on your boat.

Varnishing brightwork. Polishing a hull. Shining brass or stainless steel. Oiling or sanding wood. Most boaters spend time at dock maintaining the exterior of their boat. At dock, it's easy for chemicals to drip into the water or for the chemically treated wood dust to find its way there. Skirting the hull is a simple step that boaters can take to reduce the likelihood of toxins entering the water from the exterior work.

Skirting takes little time and simply involves running a line of tape lengthwise along the hull and affixing to it a tarp or sheet of plastic that's draped down to the dock surface where it's secured by a weight. The skirt will block any liquid spills and some dust from entering the water.

Whether you're using a dustless sander or not, if you're going to be sanding, moisten the tarp a little to cause the wood dust to congeal to the surface and prevent the wind from spreading it. After you've finished your project, you can roll down the tarp and dispose of it on land in an appropriate manner.

Other Steps You Can Take at Dock

- Limit the amount of work involving sanding and harsh chemicals to the times that you haul out your boat and have it in a yard.
- Check with your marina about what maintenance activities are permitted at dock.

- Use a dustless sander. (see chapter 35 on dustless sanding.)
- Have a spill kit ready. Have one or two oil-absorbent pads ready on the dock in case of a small drip or spill of a product that can be captured by the pad. (See chapter 11 on making up a spill kit.)
- Always wear protective gear (gloves, an appropriate breathing mask, goggles) when working around toxic chemicals.

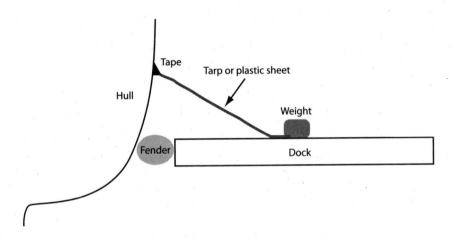

Fig. 34.1: *Skirting a boat at dock.*

CHAPTER 35

Use a Dustless Sander

A dustless sander keeps residue from entering the water.

From bottom painting to removing old varnish, many boat jobs involve sanding or even sand-blasting. Boaters haul out to do large jobs like painting the bottom, but smaller jobs like varnishing are often done at dock. The products used to keep the bottoms of our vessels unfouled and our topside teak looking nice are toxic. They don't belong in our air or our water. Normal sanders release the material they remove into the atmosphere from where it finds its way into the water. Dustless sanders use vacuum action to suck what they remove into a container, which can be emptied in an approved hazardous waste facility. Dustless sanders eliminate nearly 99% of all particulate matter they dislodge, which means not only does the environment benefit, but you benefit by not breathing in these harmful substances.

Steps You Can Take

- Invest in a small dustless sander for jobs that you do at dockside. Some marinas have regulations that prevent sanding with the exception of using a dustless sander.
- Ask your yacht club or boating association to invest in a dustless sander that will be community property for all members to use.
- If you don't belong to a club or association, ask boaters along your dock if they'd like to invest in a community dustless sander.
- Ask your marina or port authority to invest in a dustless sander that boaters can use at a nominal fee. Funds may be available to your

marina for purchase of such items through programs such as the Clean Marina Program.

- Ask your boatyard to invest in dustless sanders.
- While at dock, skirt your boat even if using a dustless sander. This will provide maximum protection for the water.
- Use gloves and an approved respirator whenever sanding, even if using a dustless sander. Particulate matter can aggravate or cause respiratory problems.

Dustless Sander Success Stories

Port Annapolis, Maryland, won the 2003 Marina of the Year Award. Part of its program included dustless sanders they purchased then provided to boaters for do-it-yourself projects.

Lake of the Ozarks, in central Missouri, is a 95-mile-long inland private lake owned by the Union Electric Company. More than 70,000 boats are docked around the lake, and there are two state parks. It is a zero-discharge lake, and the Lodge of the Four Seasons Marina allows no outside contractors or do-it-yourselfers. In 1995 the Marina invested several thousand dollars in two dustless sanders. They soon realized huge savings, cutting 30% off the time typically spent to prep a boat for a bottom job, saving boaters an average $205 on the cost of a bottom job, and reducing by 90% the labor involved in ground cleanup.

Dustless sanders are part of the mix of practices and equipment that helped Deep River Marina along the Connecticut River win the National Marine Manufacturers' Association's first Boating Facilities Environmental Responsibility Award in 1993. Their actions were good not only for the environment, but also for the marina's bottom line. From savings and increased business because of their high environmental standards, the marina saw an increase in profit from their investment in the environment.[1]

FOR THE ENJOYMENT AND PROTECTION OF OUR WATERS

MARYANNE JESSEN

CHAPTER 36

Boating on Environmental Credit

Offset the impact of boating by purchasing carbon credits.

One answer to the contribution of carbon emissions (greenhouse gases) to global warming and the degradation of the environment has been to develop a carbon credit program where anyone can purchase credits to offset their carbon footprint. The system is simple:

1. Compute the amount of carbon dioxide (CO_2) created by activities like driving a car, flying in an airplane or the electrical demands of your home.
2. Convert that amount into a dollar amount that you purchase from an organization that uses your funds for programs like reforestation, which helps to sequester CO_2, and conversion to clean and renewable energy, which helps to reduce the buildup of CO_2.

Carbon credits are not the final answer to global warming or environmental degradation, but they can help. So, what's our carbon footprint as boaters?

Carbon calculators exist for many human activities, but not yet for boating. There are many factors that come into play in calculating the amount of CO_2 produced by a boat — including engine size, age, fuel type, average cruising speed, fuel efficiency and number of hours the engine is run. Boat engines usually produce more CO_2 than automobile engines of the same type. Still, using the figures to calculate automobile carbon footprints will certainly provide an estimate of how much carbon boats create.

Calculating Your Carbon Footprint As a Boater

Using figures from the British firm Climate Care, the formula for calculating your carbon footprint is:

- **For diesel engines**: Hours of Engine Use x Fuel Burned per Hour x 0.013 = Tons of Carbon Produced

  For example, a diesel engine is in use 200 hours per year and burns 6 gal. per hour at the boat's average cruising speed. That boater's annual carbon footprint would then be:

$$200 \text{ x } 6 \text{ x } 0.013 = 15.6 \text{ tons of carbon}$$

- **For gasoline engines**: Hours of Engine Use x Fuel Burned per Hour x 0.011 = Tons of Carbon Produced

  A gasoline engine is in use 200 hours per year but burns 10 gal. per hour at the boat's average cruising speed. That boater's annual carbon profile would be:

$$200 \text{ x } 10 \text{ x } 0.011 = 22.0 \text{ tons of carbon}$$

Compute the Carbon Credit

Once you know your boat's carbon footprint, compute an approximate carbon credit equivalent by multiplying by $16 per ton of carbon. So, for the first boater in our example above:

$$15.6 \text{ tons of carbon x } \$16.00 \text{ per ton} = \$250 \text{ per year}$$

For the second boater with the gasoline engine, the carbon credit equivalent would be:

$$22 \text{ tons of carbon x } \$16 \text{ per ton} = \$352 \text{ per year}$$

How to Purchase Carbon Credits

The carbon credit business has grown tremendously in the last few years. As with any start-up industry, standards and practices vary. Examine the organizations you're interested in supporting and choose one that has clearly stated objectives for using your carbon credit. Seek out organizations that do more than simply plant trees with the carbon credits that you purchase from them. Look for organizations that make diversified use of your funds and, in particular, devote some of their resources to the marine environment. Of course, you do not have to purchase credits from an organization that specializes in carbon credit exchange. You can simply compute your carbon credits and donate that much to any organization working toward the benefit of the marine environment.

Your Carbon Credit Calculator

Fill-in the following information for the engines on your boat:

Carbon credit calculation form

1. Number of diesel engines aboard my boat   _____

2. Combined fuel burned per hour
   for all diesel engines   _____

3. Hours of use per year for all diesel engines   _____

4. Total diesel fuel consumed each year   _____

5. My carbon footprint from diesel engines   multiply result of   _____tons of CO_2
   step 4 by 0.013

6. Number of gasoline engines aboard
   my boat   _____

7. Combined fuel burned per hour for
   all gasoline engines   _____

8. Hours of use per year for all
   gasoline engines   _____

9. Total gasoline fuel consumed each year   _____

10. My carbon footprint from   Multiply result of   _____tons of CO_2
    gasoline engines   step 9 by 0.011

11. My combined carbon footprint   Add the result of   _____tons of CO_2
    step 5 and step 10

12. Cost of my carbon credit   Multiply result of
    step 11 by $16.00 $ _____

Fig. 36.1

Carbon Neutral Is Just One Step

Becoming a carbon neutral boater is just one step toward protecting the environment in general and the marine environment specifically. While it's an easy step to take, and you should be congratulated if you choose to take it, remember that we still need to employ as many other methods of environmentally sound boating as we can.

Remember, once you know your carbon footprint from boating (or any other activity), you can offset it by donating to any organization working to promote positive environmental change.

Organizations That Promote Carbon Credits

Climate Care
115 Magdalen Road Oxford
United Kingdom OX4 1RQ
Tel: +44 (0)1865 207 000 Fax: +44 (0)1865 201 900
www.climatecare.org
mail@climatecare.org

Conservation International
2011 Crystal Drive, Suite 500
Arlington, VA 22202
(703) 341-2400
Toll-free: 1(800) 429-5660
www.conservation.org

Offsetters Carbon Neutral Society
15-555 West 12th Avenue
Vancouver BC
Canada V5Z 3X0
www.offsetters.ca

Internet Search Term
"carbon footprint"; "carbon credits"; "carbon footprint calculator"

CHAPTER 37

Enjoy Safe Encounters with Marine Mammals

Boating precautions can help protect marine mammals.

B oaters share the marine environment with many other living creatures. Encountering a whale, a porpoise, a seal or a manatee is an exciting experience, one that draws many boaters to the water. It's easy to forget that our presence around these magnificent creatures can be disruptive. Like humans, they need space to find food, to mate, to raise their young, to interact with each other and to rest. The noise from our engines, the speed of our boats or our very presence amongst them can create stress, interfering with activities vital to their survival. There are no laws governing human interaction with marine mammals, other than that humans should not disturb or harass them. Here are some specific guidelines for safe encounters.

Whales

BE CAUTIOUS and COURTEOUS. Approach areas of known or suspected marine mammal activity with extreme caution. Look in all directions before planning your approach or departure. SLOW DOWN. Reduce speed to less than 7 knots when within 400 meters/yards of the nearest whale. Avoid abrupt course changes.

AVOID approaching closer than 100 meters/ yards to any whale. If whales are curious, they'll come to you.

STOP IMMEDIATELY if your vessel is unexpectedly within 100 meters/yards of a whale, and allow the whales to pass.

AVOID approaching whales from the front or from behind. Always approach and depart whales from the side, moving in a direction parallel to the direction of the whales.

KEEP CLEAR of the whales' path. Avoid positioning your vessel within the 400 meter/yard area in the path of the whales.

STAY on the OFFSHORE side of the whales when they are traveling close to shore. Remain at least 200 meters/yards offshore at all times.

LIMIT your viewing time to a recommended maximum of 30 minutes. This will minimize the cumulative impact of many vessels and give consideration to other viewers.

DO NOT swim with or feed whales.[1]

Porpoises and Dolphins

OBSERVE all guidelines for watching whales.

DO NOT drive through groups of porpoises or dolphins for the purpose of bow-riding.

REDUCE SPEED gradually and avoid sudden course changes should dolphins or porpoises choose to ride the bow wave of your vessel.

Seals, Sea Lions and Birds on Land

AVOID approaching closer than 100 meters/yards to any marine mammals or birds.

SLOW DOWN and reduce your wake/wash and noise levels.

PAY ATTENTION and back away at the first sign of disturbance or agitation.

BE CAUTIOUS and QUIET when around haulouts and bird colonies, especially during breeding, nesting and pupping seasons (generally May to September).

DO NOT swim with or feed any marine mammals or birds.

Manatees

Manatees were once mistaken for mermaids. They are gentle migratory creatures that inhabit shallow, slow-moving rivers, estuaries, saltwater bays, canals and coastal areas. The West Indian manatee is concentrated in Florida during winter months, but they can be found in summer months as far west as Texas and as far north as Virginia. However, these sightings are rare. Summer sightings in Alabama, Georgia and South Carolina are common. West Indian manatees can also be found in the coastal and inland waterways of Central America and along the northern coast of South America, although distribution in these areas may be spotty. Approximately 2,000 to 3,000 manatees reside in Florida. You can reduce your chances of harming a manatee by following these simple guidelines.[2]

- While operating a boat, wear polarized glasses that make it much easier to see submerged objects and the swirling that occurs when a manatee dives. (This looks like a large footprint on the water's surface or a series of half-moon swirls.)
- Stay in the marked channels. Manatees have shown signs that they are avoiding heavy boat traffic areas. Channel depth reduces the likelihood of pinning or crushing manatees.
- Pole, paddle or use a trolling motor when you are near seagrass beds and shallow areas. These are prime manatee habitat and nursery beds for game fish and other marine life.
- Slow down. Reducing boat speed gives you a greater chance to avoid a manatee when you see one. You will also increase your safety margin with other boats. Remember to post a lookout.
- Observe and follow all manatee speed zones and caution areas.
- Stay in deep water channels when boating but be aware that manatees also use these channels when traveling.
- Look for a snout, back, tail or flipper breaking the surface. A swirl or flat spot on the water is also created by the motion of the manatee's tail when it dives or swims.
- When operating a powerboat, if you see a manatee, remain a safe distance away — 50 feet is the suggested minimum. If you want to observe the manatee, cut the motor, but don't drift over the animal.

- If you like to jet-ski, water-ski or participate in high-speed water sports, choose areas that manatees do not or cannot frequent, such as land-locked lakes or waters well offshore.
- Obey posted speed zone signs and keep away from posted manatee sanctuaries.

Stash Your Trash

Recycle your litter or throw it in a proper trash container. Debris in waterways, such as discarded plastic bags or six-pack holders, is dangerous to manatees and other forms of wildlife. Discard monofilament line or fishing hooks properly (better yet, recycle it!), because they are dangerous for manatees, other aquatic animals and swimmers. Discarding monofilament line into the waters is against the law in Florida.

Hands Off

Resist the urge to feed manatees or give them water. Not everyone loves manatees; feeding or giving them water could encourage them to swim to people who might be cruel to them. Their natural feeding patterns may also be altered by encouraging them to hang around waiting for food or water. When hand-fed lettuce or water from a hose is no longer available, manatees may not know where to find or identify natural, reliable sources of food. "Look, but don't touch" is the best policy when swimming or diving. By quietly observing manatees from a distance, you will get a rare opportunity to see the natural behavior of this unique animal. Any other actions might be considered harassment, which is against the law.

Internet Search Terms
"marine mammal protection"; "marine mammals" "safe encounters"

CHAPTER 38

Boat Green with Pets

You and your pets can enjoy and protect our waters.

M any boat owners are also pet owners. It's not uncommon at even the remotest anchorage to see a dog owner fight wind and waves in a dinghy to get to shore so that Fido can "do his business." Just like us, our pets affect our marine environment. Learning how to protect your pet while also protecting the marine environment means that you can boat green with your pets.

It's easiest to think about boating green with pets in three ways: on a boat, in the water and on the land. In each instance, you might want to observe some simple rules and precautions for the health and safety of your pet, your crew and the marine environment.

Pets Aboard

- Order an ID tag for your pet that includes your boat's permanent marina location and slip number as well as a phone contact for when you're afloat. Or consider having an ID microchip implanted in your pet. The chip, about the size of a grain of rice, is inserted at the scruff of the neck and contains a number linked to a national registry.

- Have your pet fitted for a personal flotation device (PFD).

Regardless of how good a swimmer your pet is, a sudden dunking can cause panic, and a brightly colored life jacket with a handle on top will make the animal easier to see and retrieve.

- Acclimate your pet to the PFD in small steps. Begin with a few minutes in the backyard, then on a walk, then maybe in a pool.
- Teach your dog basic safety commands, such as "on boat," "off boat," "stay" and "sit." Good luck finding any verbal command a cat will pay attention to.
- Obtain seasickness medication for your pet if necessary. While the same medications used for humans — Benadryl, Bonine, Dramamine — also work for pets, consult your vet before medicating your pet.
- Don't let animals take refuge in the V-berth — that's where motion is felt most. A nest of secured cushions or a carrier near the boat's center of motion will help skittish pets feel safe.
- Introduce your pet to the boat in incremental steps. Ideally, begin the exposure when the animal is young. Start with a day outing, then a weekend, then maybe a week-long cruise.
- Provide traction on deck over polished wooden and fiberglass surfaces.
- Tether your pet in a secure area on a short lead, keeping it away from vital equipment and clear of access needed by the crew.
- If whales or dolphins or seals approach your boat, make sure your pet is tethered.
- If the presence of large mammals in the water excites your dog and causes it to bark and become aggressive, you might want to restrain it below decks. An aggressive dog can turn an inquisitive whale into an aggressive animal in response.
- Provide steps or ramps for dogs that have trouble navigating companionway ladders.
- Provide a shady place so your pet can get out of the sun, and find a way to protect its paw pads from hot decks by either cooling the deck with water or making a piece of nonskid carpet available.
- Make sure your pet has a chance to exercise. If you're heading out for a day trip, exercise your dog before leaving the dock.
- Neither pet waste nor human waste belongs in our oceans. While aboard, dispose of pet waste in your marine sanitation device instead of tossing it overboard.

- Treat cat litter as hazardous material. Do not throw overboard if possible. If you can separate your cat's feces from the cat litter, dispose of it in your marine head.

Pets in the Water

Since you don't want your pet to fall overboard, you should take steps to prevent that happening, and also practice for that eventuality. Apart from the steps mentioned above, you might want to consider:

- Teach your pet about the properties of water. Dip their paws in it. On calm days, the water around the boat can look like an inviting shiny floor.
- Be alert even at the dock because, surprisingly, that's where many accidents happen.
- Practice swimming and rescue drills with your pet. Have a rescue plan worked out beforehand. Practice pet-overboard drills on a nice day, when it's "play," so owner and pet know the procedure.
- Consider enrolling your dog in a program that offers many levels of training from basic water safety to advanced rescue, where your dog can learn to participate in the rescue of humans who fall overboard. Your dog can earn a merit badge for each level of water safety.
- Have a large fishnet with a long handle at the ready to scoop up a pet in the water.
- Affix a piece of carpet to the stern and bow so a cat might claw its way out of the water to safety.[1]

Pets Ashore

In many of the remote places you may visit by boat, both you and your pet are non-native species. It's important to keep this in mind as you take your dog ashore.

- Keep your dog on leash when you're onshore in a remote environment.
- Carry a plastic bag and pick up whatever your dog leaves behind. Dispose of dog feces in your boat's head.
- Don't allow your dog to interact with other animals onshore, especially large mammals like sea lions, wolves, bears or cougars. This is another reason to keep your dog on a leash. You may have the best-trained animal in the world, but when face-to-face with a wild animal, your

pet's instincts may override its training with disastrous results for you, your pet or the wild animal.

- Don't allow your dog to chase or harass wildlife. To your dog it may be play, but to the wildlife it's a threat that puts additional stress on them.
- Likewise, be aware that your small dog may look like a tasty meal to a coyote, wolf, cougar or even an eagle. It's another reason to keep dogs close and on a short leash.
- Your dog's bark is a form of noise pollution for native species. It can signal danger and disrupt them from their normal activities like sitting on eggs, foraging for food or mating. If your dog can't help itself and wants to announce its presence, you may wish to muzzle the dog while ashore.
- Onshore plants are also sensitive. Don't allow your pet to dig up or trample down native plants.

Resources

Boating with Pets. Online forum for pet owners who boat. BoatUS: my.boatus.com/forum/forum_topics.asp?FID=112

Pet Programs. Online reference for pet training programs, including water safety training programs for dogs: www.boatus.com/pets/programs.asp

Internet Search Terms

"boating with pets"; "water safety" training dogs

CHAPTER 39

Protect the Water's Bottom

Anchoring is an art we can perfect to protect the water's bottom.

Our boat's engine or sail gets us to beautiful places; our boat's anchor allows us to stay there. While anchoring is an art that many boaters enjoy perfecting, it can also be harsh on the water's bottom. Anchors disrupt sea life, and continuous anchoring in popular spots can create barren areas. Fortunately, there are steps we can take that minimize our impact on ocean, river and lake beds.

The Impact of Anchoring

- Lowering and raising an anchor dislodges bottom sediment, which is an important home for aquatic life. Dislodging toxic sediment spreads pollutants that have found their way to the bottom.
- Lowering and raising an anchor or swinging at anchor can destroy wide swathes of seagrass, an important habitat for small fish and other marine life.
- Anchoring over coral can dislodge and kill this vital member of the marine ecosystem, destroying the habitat of all those creatures that depend on it.
- Anchoring can damage or destroy marine vertebrates that live on the bottom.
- Modern mooring buoys in popular anchorages can help preserve the sea floor and allow it to heal and regenerate from previous damage.
- Marine Protected Areas (MPAs) have been designated worldwide where anchoring is either prohibited or tightly regulated.

US Nautical Chart No. 1 References to Bottom Conditions

	DESCRIPTION	NOTES
S	Sand	Best choice for anchoring.
St	Stones	
G	Gravel	
Rk: rky	Rock; Rocky	
Co	Coral and Coralline algae	Don't anchor here.
Sh	Shells	
SIM	Two layers, eg. Sand over mud	
Wd	Weed (including Kelp)	Avoid.
Kelp	Kelp, Seaweed	Avoid.
K	Kelp	Avoid.
Grs	Grass	Avoid.
Stg	Sea-tangle	Any of a variety of kelp, some edible. Avoid.
Fr	Foraminifera	Tiny chambered-shell aquatic animals that feed on diatoms and bacteria. Avoid.
Gl	Globigerina	Small, chambered-shell aquatic animals whose dead shells, falling to the bottom, make up a large part of the soft mud. Avoid.
Di	Diatoms	Single-celled algae. Avoid.
Rd	Radiolaria	Tiny, shelled marine animals with small projecting spines from their shells. Avoid.
Pt	Pteropods	Mollusks. Avoid.
Pa	Polyzoa	Also called sea moss. Small marine or freshwater animals that form colonies that attach to underwater rocks and seaweed. Avoid.
Cii	Cirripedia	Crustaceans, including barnacles. Avoid.
FLi	Fucus	Tough, leathery seaweed. Avoid.

Fig. 39.1

Steps You Can Take

- Know the bottom of any area that you are considering anchoring in. Read your chart. Know the chart symbols that specify bottom type. See Figure 39.1.

- Don't anchor over coral, seagrass or kelp beds, if possible. Anchor over a sandy bottom whenever possible.
- Learn the characteristics of your ground tackle and your boat so that you can anchor quickly and safely with minimal damage to the bottom from dragging while attempting to anchor.
- Use the proper anchor scope for the depth of water. Don't just let out rode. Read your depth sounder and measure the amount of rode based on whether you need 1:3, 1:5 or 1:7 scope.
- Stern-tie when you can. It's less harmful on the water's bottom because your boat swings less. Whenever you stern-tie, try to tie up to a ring, a rock, a piece of driftwood ashore, an old logging cable. While this is less damaging to aquatic life, it can permanently scar trees that are used as shore attachment points.
- Use mooring buoys whenever possible.
- Use a marine plant and animal guide to learn about the various forms of life whose habitat you're sharing when you anchor.

Internet Search Terms
"seagrass" boats anchor; anchoring "seabed" "environmental protection" boats

CHAPTER 40

Leave No Wake, No Trace Behind

Adopt this wilderness ethic when going ashore.

A fter spending hours in the confined spaces of your vessel, what could be more exhilarating than anchoring, dropping the dinghy and heading off on an excursion to shore? It's a chance to stretch your legs, walk your dog, let the kids play, see interesting plants and wildlife, encounter stunning vistas — it's one of the major reasons that we boat. Boats can take us to remote areas that humans seldom visit. Advances in navigational technology make it possible to safely arrive at wilderness areas that are not even well charted. But with these awesome opportunities comes an equally awesome responsibility to leave the areas we visit as pristine as they were before we got there.

There's a long-standing wilderness ethic, "Leave no trace behind," that asks travelers in backcountry areas to strive to leave the absolute minimum impact on the land they visit. With only slight modification, we boaters can strive to leave little evidence of our excursions to the shore. I call this boater's ethic, "Leave no wake, no trace behind."

Eight Principles of Leave No Wake, No Trace Behind

1. Plan ahead and prepare
2. Travel and camp on durable surfaces
3. Dispose of waste properly
4. Leave what you find
5. Minimize campfire impacts
6. Respect wildlife

7. Be considerate of other boaters and visitors
8. Don't anchor on top of other boats

Plan Ahead and Prepare

Whether you're going ashore for ten minutes to walk your dog or all day for a hike, take time to plan accordingly, particularly in remote wilderness areas.

- What safety equipment, clothing, food and water will you need?
- Have you checked the weather forecast?
- Are there any regulations or restrictions that exist for the land you wish to visit?
- Do private land boundaries exist?
- Is the area part of ceremonial or sacred land claimed by an indigenous group?
- What are the skill levels and fitness of each person in your party?
- Do you have prior knowledge of the terrain and wildlife you can reasonably expect to encounter ashore? This can be gained from guidebooks, land managers and local residents.

While such planning and preparedness may at first seem to have little to do with environmental protection, resource managers report that unprepared visitors to remote areas are more likely to degrade wilderness resources and place themselves at risk.

Travel and Camp on Durable Surfaces

Camping? I thought we were boating!

Our vessels are not always our homes away from home. Many boaters have smaller vessels or children aboard. All cruise together during the day, then split up at night with some crew camping ashore. For hand-powered vessels like kayaks, or small sailboats with no inside cabin space, it's not a question of whether to camp or not — camping is an integral part of the boating experience.

By using durable surfaces, the "Leave no wake, no trace behind" ethic means choosing places to walk or camp that present minimal damage to the surrounding environment. Durable surfaces include established trails and campsites, rock, gravel, dry grasses or snow. Protect the shoreline areas of lakes, streams, rivers and the ocean by camping at least 200 feet away. Find good campsites, don't make them. Altering a site is not necessary.

In popular areas:

- Concentrate use on existing trails and campsites.
- Walk single file in the middle of the trail, even when wet or muddy.
- Keep campsites small. Focus activity in areas where vegetation is absent.

In pristine areas:

- Disperse use to prevent the creation of campsites and trails.
- Avoid places where impacts are just beginning.

Dispose of Waste Properly

- Pack it in, pack it out. Inspect your campsite and rest areas for trash or spilled foods. Pack out all trash, leftover food and litter.
- Deposit solid human waste in catholes dug 6 to 8 inches deep at least 200 feet from water, camp and trails. Cover and disguise the cathole when finished. It helps to carry a small shovel or trowel for this purpose.
- Pack out toilet paper and hygiene products. It helps to carry plastic bags for this purpose, then dispose of the contents once you get back to your boat.
- To wash yourself or your dishes, carry water 200 feet away from streams or lakes and use small amounts of biodegradable soap. Scatter strained dishwater.
- Near-shore lakes are often popular places for boaters to take a dip and wash themselves. In popular areas this can create eutrophication and dead zones. Some lakes have signage preventing boaters from washing themselves. Instead of lathering up and taking a swim, carry a bucket with you. Fill the bucket up with lake water. Carry the bucket 200 feet away from the lake (or stream). Wash and lather there.

Leave What You Find

Bring a camera with you to record the beauty you witness, but leave it there for others to behold as well.

- Preserve the past: examine, but do not touch, cultural or historic structures and artifacts.

- Leave rocks, plants and other natural objects as you find them.
- Avoid introducing or transporting non-native species.
- Do not build structures or furniture or dig trenches.

Minimize Campfire Impacts

What could be more enjoyable than sitting around a campfire ashore on a starry night? But fires can scar and damage pristine wilderness areas.

- Campfires can cause lasting impacts to the backcountry. Use a light-weight stove for cooking and enjoy a candle lantern for light.
- Where fires are permitted, use established fire rings, fire pans or mound fires if they are available.
- Keep fires small. Only use sticks from the ground that can be broken by hand.
- Smaller fires mean less chance of blowing embers igniting a larger blaze.
- Burn all wood and coals to ash, put out campfires completely, then scatter cool ashes.

Respect Wildlife

You're a visitor in their home.

- Observe wildlife from a distance. Avoid following or approaching them.
- Alter your course if you encounter larger mammals. Don't force them to alter theirs.
- Never feed animals. Feeding wildlife damages their health, alters natural behaviors and exposes them to predators and other dangers.
- Protect wildlife and your food by storing rations and trash securely. This is particularly true if you are camping or hiking in bear country.
- Control pets at all times, or leave them at home.
- Avoid wildlife during sensitive times: mating, nesting, raising young or in winter.
- Never touch an animal that appears to be stranded ashore. Some mother animals, such as seals, will intentionally strand their young ashore for protection from predators while they hunt for food. Touching a seal pup can leave a trace scent that will cause its mother to reject it and leave it to die.

Be Considerate of Other Boaters and Visitors

Several years ago, I pulled into a remote anchorage and settled in for a relaxing few days. In the past, I'd heard wolf packs howling here and seen black bears foraging along the shore. Soon after I anchored, another boater anchored in the cove. What a surprise when several minutes after anchoring, he pulled out a trumpet, stepped onto the cockpit and sent a barrage of off-key notes blaring throughout the cove. As this cacophony raged, I lowered my dinghy and rowed over to the frustrated musician. Once I got his attention, I asked him if he intended to practice all weekend. If he was, I said, I wanted to know so I could weigh anchor and find a quiet place. He did apologize, and I only heard muted trumpet sounds from below decks after that.

Many boaters are considerate of others, but not all. Be a boater who allows others to enjoy their boating experience.

- Respect other visitors and boaters by protecting the quality of their experience.
- Be courteous. Yield to other users on the trail.
- Step to the downhill side of the trail when encountering pack stock.
- Take breaks and camp away from trails and other visitors.
- Let nature's sounds prevail. Avoid loud voices and noises. Minimize generator usage. If you have to run a generator at anchor, do it during the day and not at night.

Don't Anchor on Top of Other Boats

What is it that causes other boaters to anchor so close when there's absolutely no reason?

I'd no sooner pulled into a popular anchorage along the Inside Passage and set my anchor, when a sailboat under power cruised into the spot. The skipper tossed out his anchor line and kept motoring until the line came to the bitter end. He was far too close to other boats. He didn't back down on the anchor. He just disappeared below. Early the next morning, I heard a loud thump on my hull. Sure enough, as the tide fell, that sailboat had drifted into me. I pounded on the hull to wake the skipper. He poked his head from the cabin door, rubbing his eyes. He glared at me as though I was at fault. But he pulled up his anchor and motored away into the dawn.

Most seasoned boaters have stories about the herd mentality that seems to captivate other boaters when choosing an anchor site. It's as though your boat has a large bull's eye painted on it, or a neon sign that reads, "Anchor here." In an anchorage large enough to accommodate many boats, some boaters feel compelled to anchor nearby others. It's not courteous. It's not safe. It's not necessary. And it detracts from the enjoyment of the boating experience. When you have the option, choose to anchor as far away from other boats as possible. This also reduces the impact on underwater plant and animal life.

Anchor so that you give yourself swinging room. Be extra cautious. Don't assume that the wind is the only predictor of where to anchor. I have anchored with the wind and with other surrounding boats only to find that when the wind died off, the current took over sending previously well-aligned boats helter-skelter around the anchorage and sending some into each other.

Internet Search Term
"Leave No Trace Behind"

CHAPTER 41

Chart a Course to Boat Green

Charts and reference cards can help you
protect marine environment.

W ithout navigation charts, we couldn't cruise safely. They indicate hazards, best passage routes and safe anchorages. But navigation charts can also help us boat green. On your paper charts, write in important locations that you should know about to boat green (see suggestions below). On computerized charts, use your software to mark these locations electronically. This way, while cruising, you can access information that you need to avoid sensitive wildlife areas, locate pump-out facilities and patronize marinas that are working to protect the marine environment.

Steps You Can Take

- Mark marinas that have been certified under the Clean Marina Program. See chapter 45.
- Mark all areas that are designated "No pump-out."
- Mark all locations that have pump-out facilities. See chapter 17.
- Mark "dead zone" areas. See chapter 3.
- Mark areas that are designated as Marine Protection Areas (MPAs) or National Wildlife Reserves (NWRs).

Create a Boat Green Reference Card

For your home port, create a reference card that lists important numbers and other information that you should have at your fingertips

Place the card in a prominent place, perhaps next to the required plaque about not dumping oil. The card might look something like this:

Boat green reference card

BOAT GREEN REFERENCE CARD		
Local marina	Harbormaster's Office NNN-NNNNN	M-F, 8-5 S & S, 8-6 (Summer only)
To report an oil spill	National Response Center 800-424-8802	24/7/365
Local hazardous waste disposal location	County Hazardous Waste NNN-NNN-NNNN 1234 Fairhaven Parkway	M-F, 8-4 Sat, 10-3
Local Coast Guard station	Station Zulu NNN-NNNNN 2323 Harbor Drive CO Master Chief Fred Kern	24/7/365
State Environmental Protection Department	Washington Department of Environmental Protection 800-NNN-NNNN	M-F, 8-5
State Department of Wildlife and Natural Resources	Washington Department of Natural Resources 800-NNN-NNNN	M-F, 8-5
List any other important agencies, organizations, businesses related to marine environmental protection	Institution's Name, Address, Phone Number, Contact Person	Hours of operation

Fig. 41.1

Now, when you're contemplating an oil change during the off-season months, you can easily coordinate the time of your oil change with the availability of a facility (your local marina or a local hazardous waste disposal site) to take your used oil.

Resources

To mark your chart or compile a reference card, contact the following locations for the information you need:

- Local marina or port authority
- Local coast guard station
- State department of environmental protection
- State department of wildlife or natural resources
- Recycling hotlines
- Relevant sections of this book

IN YOUR COMMUNITY

MARY JANE JESSEN

CHAPTER 42

Form an Environmental Committee within Your Club

Make boat green a part of your boating association.

Yacht clubs and boating associations traditionally have a number of standing committees to handle membership, fundraising, educational programs and cruises. Add an environmental committee to your club or association. Let that committee chair be the point person for gathering information about environmentally responsible boating, for reporting to the club the latest news about environmentally responsible boating and for planning environmental boating events for club members.

Tasks for an environmental committee

Change your club's bylaws to make an environmental committee one of the organization's standing committees. Vote on the committee's name: the Boat Green committee, the Clean Boating committee, the Eco Boating committee or some other name that club members suggest. As the first task of the newly formed environmental committee, reword the organization's mission statement to include a clause with a commitment to environmentally responsible boating. Here's an example:

Old Statement: The mission of the Fair Harbor Yacht Club is to encourage and foster the sport of yachting, the art of yacht design and construction, the science of seamanship and navigation, and to provide for the enjoyment and recreation of its members.

New Statement: The mission of the Fair Harbor Yacht Club is to encourage and foster the sport of yachting, the art of yacht design and construction, the science of seamanship and navigation, the steward-ship of the marine environment, and to provide for the enjoyment and recreation of its members.

Further tasks for the environmental committee:

- Keep a list of new boating products and services that promote marine environmental protection.
- Organize at least one Boat Green cruise each season. See the section on Adopting a Waterway for suggestions.
- Present a special program for opening day on some aspect of environmental boating. See the section on sponsoring a Green Boating Drive.
- Earmark a percentage of the association's annual budget to sponsoring an environmental boating project.
- Research and select several potential marine environmental steward-ship projects.
- Present the merits of each project to the membership before the club votes on which one to support.
- Organize a hands-on demonstration of environmentally sound boating practices: good fueling techniques, the quirks of using the port or marina's pump-out facility, how to skirt a boat. Thumb through the pages of this book for more ideas about activities the environmental committee can undertake.
- Develop an environment burgee or flag that incorporates some aspect of green boating with the association's existing burgee. Donate the proceeds of sales of that burgee to an organization working to protect the marine environment.
- Organize a special evening demonstration and discount purchase opportunity at a local chandlery. Tell the chandlery that you'd like to see a special display of environmentally friendly boating products.
- Develop a special award that's given each year to a member who demonstrates commitment to the protection of marine environment.

Appoint the committee's chairperson as the club's liaison to the environmental manager of the port or marina where the club is located. Invite the environmental manager to speak at one of your regular meetings. The chairperson will also be the club's liaison to other area environmental groups. Invite a member of one of those groups to speak at a regular meetings. It's a great way to build bridges between the boating and the environmental community.

CHAPTER 43

Host a Boat Green Event

Involve the boating community in educational presentations.

B oaters are always hungry for information and education that will help improve their experience and enjoyment of being on the water. If that information and education also benefits the environment it's a win-win situation. If you can plan a party, you can host a boat green event. But be forewarned, when word gets out that you're putting on an event that will talk about boating safety, boating equipment and performance, boat maintenance and enjoyment of the boating, be ready for a standing-room-only crowd.

Planning a Boat Green Event

Select a set of topics for your event, three at most, that will hold boaters' attention for at least two hours. You might want to select three topics from this book that will interest most boaters. Choose topics that cut across the spectrum of boating, like biodiesel, which can be used by sailboaters and powerboaters alike, or bilge maintenance, which is common to all boaters. Then follow these steps:

- Contact a national boating group working for the protection of the marine environment and ask if they have any pre-planned material on hosting an event like this. See chapter 49 for a contact list of such organizations.
- Pick a date for your event. Remember the boating season generally runs from May until September, and most boaters are either on the water or thinking about being on the water. So, plan your event

sometime between October and April, especially March and April when boaters are thinking about the maintenance and care needed for the upcoming season.

- To enlist the support of a local yacht club or boating group, even if you are not a member, tell them about your plans. Chances are they'll want to pitch in and help you sponsor it and may even provide the venue.
- Talk to your marina or harbor administration. They too may want to help you pull off a successful event. They may list your event in an upcoming newsletter sent to all boaters or give you a discounted rate on renting space at a marina facility.
- Select a location near a marina or port. Part of the camaraderie of boating comes from being around boats.
- Layout a program. Allow between 30 and 45 minutes for each presentation.
- If you're not comfortable presenting the topics you've selected for the event, find someone who may have some expertise in the area. Ask around local marine businesses or at your local chandlery.
- Ask local businesses that have products related to the presentations if they would support the event financially in exchange for the opportunity to display their wares at the event.
- Ask local environmental groups if they would like to send a representative to make a short presentation. Make sure the groups you contact have both interest and expertise in marine environmental protection and know something about the needs of boaters. If they don't, contact them anyway but invite them to listen and learn rather than to speak.
- If possible, develop a website with information about the event.
- Get the word out locally through flyers and newspaper ads.
- Learn how to write a public service announcement (PSA) about your event. Many radio and television stations will run PSAs for free. Enter the Internet search term "How to write a PSA" to access two hundred or so pages about creating a PSA and getting it aired.
- Invite public officials: the mayor and town council, the chief of the fire department, the chief of police, the commander of your local coast guard station.
- Invite officials connected to boating: members of the port or marina administration, the head of the boat-lending section at your local bank, boat insurance brokers, boat brokers.

- Even if your event is free, make sure you have a voluntary sign-up sheet at the door so that attendees can leave you their name and e-mail address. That way you can contact them about future events.

Begin the meeting by stating the Boat Green philosophy. Feel free to put it in your own words or use the following:

> Boat Green believes that boaters are a small part of the problem of the degradation of the marine environment, but they can be a big part of the solution. We know the marine environment better than most. We love the marine environment. And most importantly, we know the needs of boaters. By taking a lead in practices that promote vessel safety, enhanced performance and decreased operating costs, while also benefiting the marine environment, boaters can demonstrate how enjoying our pastime and protecting the marine environment go hand-in-hand.

Have a simple feedback sheet where participants can tell you what they thought about the event. Their answers will provide invaluable information about the success of this event and the planning of future events. Ask straightforward questions such as:

- What did you like most about the event?
- What did you like least about the event?
- What would you like to see offered at an event like this in the future?
- Would you attend future events?
- Would you help with the planning and execution of a future event?

You can begin tentative planning for your next boat green event as soon as the first one is over. Be prepared to become the local go-to person for information and action related to boating and the marine environment.

Have copies of *Boat Green* for sale at these events. Contact the publisher for discounts on larger volumes. Use the money obtained from selling the books to offset the costs of holding the event. Or consider donating a portion of these proceeds to a group working to protect the marine environment.

CHAPTER 44

Adopt a Waterway

Make the protection of a marine resource
your personal responsibility.

D riving down a highway, we see signs telling us that a business or civic organization has adopted this stretch of road, taking responsibility for keeping it trash free and perhaps for maintaining the landscaping. Their members will sometimes organize direct participation in picking up trash or planting flowers. At other times, the organization will raise money to pay for these services. This participation of citizens provides great support to overburdened government agencies that do not have the resources to perform these functions. Boaters can adopt stretches of water in the same way. You can organize a group of boaters to adopt a river, a stream, a lake, a bay, a coast, even an island.

Steps You Can Take

Contact the Waterkeepers Alliance (see resources at the end of this section) or your state and local authorities to see if there are any high-priority resources in your area that might benefit from your efforts. If you belong to a yacht club or boating association, form a committee on marine resource adoption and have the club vote on a section of a river or lake, a stretch of coastline, a small bay or island that it would like to adopt. If you don't belong to a boating group, or your association isn't in a position to adopt a marine resource, form your own group of boating friends. Otherwise, ask a non-boating group interested in that resource if you can help as a boater.

Write up an adoption plan for the resource that you choose. Before taking any action, submit your adoption plan to state or local authorities to make sure that it does not conflict with any ongoing management of that resource. At a minimum, that adoption plan should include:

- Name of the resource.
- Latitude and longitude coordinates of resource, if appropriate.
- Name and contact information of person responsible for adoption group
- Objectives of the adoption.
- What specific activities you will engage in.

Hold a fundraising event for the adoption of the resource. Make it fun. Write up adoption papers and ask a local official to sign them, formally acknowledging your adoption of the resource. Issue a press release to your local newspaper about the adoption. Ask them to send a reporter to the ceremony.

Your adoption can also be an educational opportunity to show others what they can do to make a difference. Include the following activities:

- Hold a work day to benefit your adopted resource
- Have a cleanup cruise to pick up trash on the water or along the shore.
- Cruise to an island, if that's your adopted resource, and pick up trash there. Help to maintain the trails on the island.
- Offer to ferry environmental groups to hard-to-get-to marine locations they need to visit.
- Monitor pollution in a waterway, reporting back to local authorities any pollution that you find.
- Enlist the help of others in your cleanup efforts. Most boaters enjoy any excuse to get out on the water. Ask your local kayak club if they would like to participate. Invite a local scout troop to join you.
- Invite the public to go on a shoreline walk to pick up trash.
- Bring along non-boaters on your outing. Invite members of a local environmental group on your adoption cruises. This can be a tremendous method for building bridges between boaters and non-boaters interested in protecting our marine resources. Environmentalists often

don't understand the reality of boaters, while boaters often don't understand the perils facing the marine environment. Your adoption cruise can change that.

If you're unable to actually participate in the work that needs to be done on your adopted resource, ask your group or club to set aside a portion of its annual budget to be given to a group that will maintain that resource.

Resources

WaterkeeperAlliance 50 S. Buckhout, Suite 302 Irvington , New York 10533
  Tel: 914 674-0622 info1@waterkeeper.org
  Coordinates more than 150 Riverkeeper, Coast, Bay, Sound, Inlet, Cape,
  Channel, Creek and Shore "Keepers" programs around the world. For a
  searchable list of waterkeeper programs, or to start your own, visit their
  website: www.waterkeeper.org
See chapter 49 for a list of organizations that you can join. These organizations
  will often have local projects that you and your group can participate in.

CHapTeR 45

Work with Your Local Marina

Your local marina is a partner for boating green.

I n your local marina or port authority, you'll find a partner for boating green. Marinas are key to the recreational boating industry. They provide long-term and transient moorage, access to marine businesses and services that boaters require and must comply with local, state and federal environmental protection standards. Furthermore, you are their customer. What matters to you should matter to them.

Marinas can assist boaters in boating green in many ways: through providing pump-out and hazardous waste disposal sites; making expensive tools such as dustless sanders available to boaters for a nominal fee; providing education and information on environmental best practices for boaters; and supporting the efforts of boating associations located at the marina.

Did You Know

There are an estimated 8,000 to 10,000 marinas in the United States. A 1996 study of 25 of these marinas showed that:

- Every marina had active solid waste management and public education programs.
- All but one had pump-out stations and were promoting their use. Most had issued marina no-discharge regulations. Eight were highlighted for the way they promoted or used pump-out service.
- Nearly 90 percent have been involved in shoreline stabilization, storm water runoff control, liquid material management and petroleum control.

- Over 70 percent have improved their fuel docks and boat-cleaning practices.
- Some marinas are actively involved in fish restocking programs — Oak Harbor, Washington, (Coho and Chinook salmon rearing and release), and Puerto del Rey (sea turtle rescue) — illustrating the very interesting potential for widespread habitat enhancement in marinas. And they also show that marina basins can indeed be healthy and productive ecosystems.
- Surprisingly, only 28 percent found sport-fishing activity high enough to need cleaning stations.
- Two marinas met or exceeded the requirements for all 14 of the federal coastal management measures applicable to marinas in 1993.[1]

Steps You Can Take

- If you haven't already, get to know your local marina owner or harbormaster. Say that you're interested in working with the marina to protect local waters.
- If the marina or port authority has an environmental manager, introduce yourself to that person. Say that you'd like to know how you could work together to protect the marine environment.
- List the steps you would like to see the marina take to support boating green. Tell the harbormaster or environmental manager you'd like to help accomplish them. In some cases the marina can actually apply for federal grants to upgrade its facilities to protect the marine environment.
- Invite the harbormaster or environmental manager to your boating association to talk about what the marina is doing to protect local waters and educate boaters.
- Ask your marina to become a certified "Clean Marina" by the US Environmental Protection Agency, described below.

The Clean Marina Initiative

The Clean Marina Initiative is a voluntary, incentive-based program promoted by the National Oceanic and Atmospheric Administration (NOAA) and other federal agencies like the Environmental Protection Agency that encourage marina operators and recreational boaters to protect coastal water quality by engaging in environmentally sound operating and maintenance procedures.[2] While Clean Marina Programs vary from state to state, all programs offer information, guidance and technical assistance to marina operators, local governments and recreational boaters on Best Management Practices (BMPs) that can be used to prevent or reduce pollution. Marinas that participate in the Clean Marina Program are recognized for their environmental stewardship.

Benefits for Marinas Operators and Owners

- Reduce waste disposal costs. BMPs will reduce the amount of wastes produced so disposal costs will be less.
- Generate new sources of revenue. Studies have shown that Clean Marinas can charge slightly higher slip fees and have fewer vacancies.
- Receive free technical assistance. BMP guidebooks, training workshops and onsite visits are available to marina operators. Some states will even offer onsite assistance for meeting regulatory requirements.
- Reduce legal liabilities. By participating in the Clean Marina Program, marinas can ensure they are meeting all regulatory requirements, thus avoiding fines.
- Enjoy free publicity. States recognize Clean Marinas through press releases, newsletters and boating guides, etc.
- Attract knowledgeable customers. Clean Marinas are aesthetically pleasing facilities that can attract responsible clientele who will follow good boating practices. Clean Marinas report increased business from boaters interested in protecting the marine environment.
- Improve water quality and habitat for living resources. The marina and boating industry depends on clean waters and a healthy coastal environment for their continued success.
- Demonstrate the marina is a good steward of the environment. Many states distribute special burgees and signs for Clean Marinas to display. Clean Marinas are also allowed to use the state's Clean Marina logo on all letterhead.

Resources

National Management Measures to Control Nonpoint Source Pollution from Marinas and Recreational Boating. US EPA Washington, DC. EPA 841-B-01-005. November 2001.

Shipshape Shores and Waters: A Handbook for Marina Operators and Recreational Boaters. US EPA Washington, DC. EPA-B-03-001. January 2003.

National Clean Boating Campaign. This maintains an extensive list of references and contacts on clean marinas and clean boating: cleanboating.org/bibliography/index.html

Environmental Protection Agency (EPA): www.epa.gov/owow/nps/marinas.html

SeaGrant's MarinaNet: www.sgmarinanet.org/mnet.html

Marine Environmental Education Foundation (MEEF): oceanservice.noaa.gov/cgi-bin/redirout.cgi?url=http://www.meef.org/

BoatUS Foundation: oceanservice.noaa.gov/cgi-bin/redirout.cgi?url=http://www.boatus.com/foundation

US Fish and Wildlife Service's Clean Vessel Act Program: federalaid.fws.gov/cva/cva.html

Ocean Conservancy's Good Mate Program: www.oceanconservancy.org/site/PageServer?pagename=op_goodmate

Georgia Strait Alliance's Clean Marina Program: georgiastrait.org

Ontario Marine Operators Association's Clean Marina Program: www.marinasontario.com/clean_ marine_faq.asp

Internet Search Term

"Clean Marinas"

CHaPTeR 46

Get Involved with Boating and Environmental Issues

Boaters should be informed stakeholders
in the marine environment.

Marina expansion. Shoreline development. Habitat restoration. Toxic waste cleanup. Municipal sewage. Industrial and agricultural runoff. These are some of the many issues that waterfront communities contend with today. They are related to all aspects of community life from the economy to the arts to housing. They affect the quality of life. They impact the marine environment. And they touch our experience as boaters. Politicians, environmental activists, developers and concerned citizens are frequently around the table discussing, arguing and negotiating the competing demands that these issues raise. But boaters are just as frequently absent from these interactions. Locally, regionally and nationally, we boaters are important stakeholders in the marine environment and all issues related to it. Inform yourself about important issues that affect boating and the marine environment. Take a stand. Don't be silent. Boaters' opinions count. Let your voice be heard.

Steps You Can Take

If your marina or port has an advisory committee composed of boaters, consider becoming a member. If your marina or port doesn't have an advisory committee, ask them to establish one.

Can you name the three most important issues affecting your local waterfront or favorite local boating area? If not, ask around and find out what they are. For any issue, answering these questions will help you get more involved:

- What's a brief description of the issue?
- How long has this issue been around?
- What are the contributing factors to the issue?
- Who are the various stakeholders in this local issue?
- What are their positions on the issue?
- What are the impacts of these positions on boating?
- Evaluate the issue from a boater's point of view. What's your position?
- What important decisions will be made?
- Who will make them? A city or county council? A state agency? The federal government?
- When will these decisions be made?
- In what ways can you engage in the discourse around these decisions? Attending meetings? Writing letters to your local paper? Making telephone calls or sending e-mails to local politicians? Organizing an educational event? Mounting a protest?
- After collecting this information, ask yourself: "What's the first step I should take?"

A Hypothetical Case Study

A beautiful mountain lake has been used by boaters for years. The lake is also a source of drinking water for the community along the shoreline. In recent years, more homes have been built around the lake, putting pressure on the water supply. Developers have now begun to build homes on the hillsides overlooking the lake, adding even further pressure. With no municipal sewage to the lakeside communities, all homes have septic systems with drainage fields.

Then a recent state water quality survey shows the lake is heading for trouble. Oxygen levels are down; toxic pollutant levels are up. If something is not done, the State may declare the lake unfit to use for drinking water and mandate the construction of an expensive water treatment facility at the county's expense. County officials inform local residents that if such a mandate is delivered they will be forced to raise property taxes. Citizens are up in arms over that prospect.

When an environmental group joins the fray, they observe that many boats with gasoline outboard engines regularly use the lake. They also note that most engines are older model two-stroke models. They bring out charts to show how the oil and exhaust from these engines are leading to the diminished water quality and to eutrophication of the lake. Now, there's an identifiable source of blame — boaters!

So lake residents who aren't boaters now organize a "Boats off the Lake" campaign. They want the county to declare the lake a boat-free zone. When boaters hear of this, they organize a counter-campaign, dubbed "Boats on the Lake." The two camps have acrimonious exchanges played out at county council meetings, in the local press, on local talk radio shows and through flyers posted throughout the community that read, "Boats off" or "Boats on."

Meanwhile, developers are only too happy to have local groups battling between themselves. It takes the pressure off them from responsibility for cutting down the forested areas above the lake that contribute to runoff, which degrades water quality. Politicians are also happy because the pressure is off them to find solutions. It's a lot easier to pick sides in the dispute than it is to come up with answers. There's an "Are you with me, or against me" attitude among lake residents. Neighbors no longer talk to neighbors on the other side of the issue.

What's lost in the bitterness and bickering is a perspective on finding solutions to the underlying problems that might satisfy all stakeholders involved. Here's where boaters with a boat green attitude could really make a difference by voicing opinions and proposing solutions such as:

- Boaters are not the only contributors to the degradation of lake quality. Developers contribute through deforestation and increased septic systems. Local residents contribute through allowing runoff from their driveways and fertilized lawns into the lake. So, instead of pointing the finger of blame, everyone needs to look at how they can mitigate the impact of their activities on the lake.
- Boaters with two-stroke engines should be encouraged to upgrade to four-stroke engines. Boaters with diesel engines should be encouraged to use biodiesel. Electric outboards would be even more preferable. If local residents work with state and county officials there may actually be grants they can apply for to help boaters purchase new engines.
- The marinas on the lake should apply for funds available to upgrade their facilities to provide state-of-the-art pump-out stations for all

boats. The marinas should also implement all steps to become certified Clean Marinas.

- Boater education packages should be prepared that outline simple steps boaters can take to decrease operating costs, improve performance and reduce the impact of their boating on the lake.
- Boat Green packages should be handed out to boaters. These packages would contain information and practical items such as fuel-spill cups and the highest-quality bilge socks. Federal and foundation funds may be available to purchase and distribute these packages.
- The "Boat on" and "Boat off" campaigns should disband in favor of a "Boat Green" campaign which showcases how a community can rally around an important local issue and implement innovative solutions that are a model for other communities throughout the country and around the world.

The only way we can hope for solutions like these is if boaters, passionate about boating and the environment, get involved in tough local issues like this.

Additional Steps You Can Take

- Make sure you know your local and state politicians. Ask them where they stand on issues related to boating. Are they boaters? If not, offer to take them out on your boat. Show them problems on the water from a boater's point of view. Tell them you're available to be consulted on boating issues and the environment.
- Invite local politicians to speak at your boating association meetings. It's a chance to hear their views about boating-related issues and for them to hear from a group of committed local boaters.
- If you're a writer and your local paper doesn't have a column on boating issues, offer to write one.
- Keep a separate e-mail list of contacts for all local stakeholders in the marine environment and regularly send out e-mails with your thoughts and ideas on local water issues.
- Create an Internet blog site where you write about local boating and water issues. Direct others to the site.
- Join a local, state, national or international organization working to protect the marine environment. See chapter 49 on joining such organizations.

CHAPTER 47

Teach Children the Value of Boat Green

Help raise the next generation of boaters who will protect our waters.

What could be more heartwarming than watching a parent teaching a child to fish or sitting a child behind the helm of a boat and helping them learn how to steer and work the gears. Boating is a family activity, an opportunity for families to spend quality, relaxing time together enjoying the marine environment. Children are naturally inquisitive and eager to learn under the tutelage of adults. One of the most important steps any boater can take to protect the marine environment is passing along a boat green ethic to a younger generation of boaters.

Steps You Can Take

The next time your children, grandchildren, nieces or nephews are out on your boat, make a point of talking to them about the steps you're taking to help protect the marine environment and why. Follow these steps to get your family involved:

- Let children participate in age-appropriate tasks aboard your boat that have to do with protection of the marine environment like recycling, pumping out the head or changing oil. Make sure you supervise them, and while they're performing the task, tell them what they're doing that helps to protect the waters they are enjoying.
- Bookmark cool sites for your children like the webcams of marine environmental organizations. (See list of webcams below.)

- Surf the Internet with your children, looking for organizations that are working to protect the marine environment and have items of interest to children — a kids' section, cool graphics, dazzling animations, activities that children can take part in.
- Select an Urgent Action appeal (see chapter 48 on going online to Boat Green) that you and your children can agree on. Let them sign their name to a petition or an e-mail and add their comments about why they want the marine environment protected. Their voices can have a huge impact on lawmakers and officials.

You could also contact local schools to get their students involved in the marine environment. Here's some possibilities:

- Offer your boat to take a group of children from a local middle school on an environmental cruise. Organize this trip with several boats from your yacht club.
- Speak with school officials and teachers, especially science teachers. They will assist you in organizing an educational event for the children, and they'll be grateful for your help.
- Go online and look for lesson plans that teach students about protection of the marine environment.
- Curricula are available for meaningful daylong classes that teach students about the marine environment and the importance of protecting it. If your school doesn't have the resources to develop a daylong lesson plan for teaching students about protecting the marine environment, contact a local environmental organization and enlist their help in developing such a lesson plan.
- A science teacher may want to drag an experiment behind the boat that teaches students about measuring oxygen content in the water, and about the dangers of eutrophication.
- Perhaps the students will collect water samples and then examine them under a microscope looking for what microorganisms are found there.
- Perhaps there's a nearby island where children can get off to examine the flora and fauna, see a wetland and observe the effects of pollution.
- Take the time to teach the students about what steps you take on your boat to protect the marine environment.

Resources

The National Marine Educators Association. This largest association of marine educators in the United States has chapters across the country. They publish the *Journal of Marine Education* with activities. Also a newsletter with reviews of curricular material: www.marine-ed.org

The National Oceanic and Atmospheric Administration (NOAA) website for Marine Educators:
www.mpa.gov/helpful_resources/education_training_pr.html#infoexchange.

International Pacific Marine Educators Conference. Brings together marine educators from 18 countries. Conference presentations are available for free viewing online.

For webcams from all over the world related to the marine environment, visit www.twopears.com/oceans.shtml. Also see the list of webcams related to islands and marine animals like eels and orcas.

Internet Search Terms

"marine education"; "marine education" children; "marine education" curricula; marine webcams

CHaPTeR 48

Go Online to Boat Green

The Internet offers many ways to protect our waters.

Acccess to information is a critical step in the process of making a difference and bringing about change. With the advent of the Internet, key information about the challenges and solutions of protecting our marine environment is available to any boater with a computer and a phone line. Because the amount of this information can be overwhelming, organizing how you use the Internet and understanding some of your online options can help you better use the Internet as a tool to boat green.

Steps You Can Take

There's more than one way to access the Internet:

- Don't have an Internet connection? Visit your local public library to use their Internet stations. They are often so busy that you may want to call ahead to schedule time. Also, look for local Internet cafes that have computers to rent.
- Cruising with your computer aboard but without an Internet connection? Many marinas have Internet facilities that you can use; some have wireless service that broadcasts throughout the marina. Check with the harbormaster or simply bring up your wireless network finder and see if there are any networks you can connect to.
- Don't forget your cellphone. Some cellphone companies have wireless plans that will give you Internet service wherever you have cell

service. Other Internet options for cruising boats include satellite phones with Internet access.

Use the Internet search terms and websites in this book when searching the facts on such topics as:

- The state and health of the marine environment
- The latest technologies to help boaters reduce maintenance costs, boost equipment performance, enhance safety and protect the marine environment
- Specific products such as eco-friendly cleansers and bottom paints

The Internet also helps you to communicate with other boaters and groups and to take specific actions to help protect and preserve the marine environment:

- Go online to join a group of boaters working to protect the health of the marine environment.
- Join an e-mail list (listserv) or community bulletin board where boaters trade information about products, services and technologies related to boating green. Periodically, sometimes once a day, you will receive an e-mail of the correspondence among listserv members. You can respond to the entire list as you would to a normal e-mail, and your response will become part of the ongoing online conversation. A community bulletin board is slightly different; members post messages and reply to posted messages. Frequently, you can notify the bulletin board that you would like to follow any messages and replies related to a given topic. For instance, if you're interested in everything that's being said about "biodiesel," you can tell the bulletin board and then you'll receive an e-mail every time there's correspondence on the bulletin board about biodiesel. Some of the organizations you can join have associated bulletin boards or listservs.
- Subscribe to a Really Simple Syndication (RSS) feed. Some organizations with websites also allow visitors to subscribe to RSS feeds from their website, indicated by an orange RSS sign. Clicking this symbol then places you on a list of subscribers who receive real time news from the website on their desktop computers, much like you would if you subscribed to wire service for news or a stock service for stock ticker feeds. You can pick up the RSS feed in a number of ways; most

modern e-mail programs and browsers have RSS capabilities so you can get the RSS news feeds when you get your e-mail. Similarly, most modern browsers will also receive RSS feeds. Some programs operate standalone on your desktop and broadcast the latest RSS updates independently of you fetching your e-mail. This can be a very effective means of staying current about a particular topic, for instance, to keep abreast of late-breaking news about an important piece of environmental legislation that affects your boating community.

Urgent Action appeals (UAs) are often posted on websites of organizations working to protect the marine environment. Answering a UA can be a very satisfying way of joining thousands of others who lend their voices and their money to actions aimed at making a difference and protecting our marine environment. These UAs will describe actions, such as the following, that need to be taken immediately, and also offer other simple steps that you can take to help.

- Perhaps an important piece of legislation affecting boaters is pending in Congress, and the UA will give you a telephone number to call.
- Maybe the US Coast Guard needs to hear the opinion of boaters about new regulations they are considering.
- A group working to protect the marine environment in a remote corner of the world may need the support of boaters around the world to lobby for governmental change in their home country.
- You can help by signing an e-mail petition or sending an e-mail letter to the appropriate authorities that the organization has already prepared but you can modify.
- You can donate funds to help address urgent situations.
- Use links to other websites.
- Join a listserv, bulletin board or RSS feed to receive UAs, which you can forward to other people you think may want to help.
- Ask your yacht club or boating association to respond to a UA that all agree supports the aims and goals of the club.

Resources
See related chapters of this book that deal with joining an organization working to protect the marine environment (chapter 49), hosting a boat green event (chapter 43) and any sections with Internet search terms.

Join an Organization Working for the Marine Environment

Working in a team, boaters can make a difference.

A t the local, state and national level, organizations can benefit from the support and assistance of boaters interested in promoting environmentally sound boating practices. Some of these organizations have been formed by boaters themselves; other organizations are working for the health of the marine environment without the benefit of boaters among them. Often, well-meaning environmental organizations propose regulations, develop campaigns and present educational programs without the input of boaters. Understandably, when confronted with such initiatives, boaters are skeptical because these frequently reflect a lack of boating awareness. So, join a group of boaters or non-boaters working for the protection of our waters. Let your voice be heard. Tell others what you know. Help make a difference.

There are hundreds of organizations working worldwide to protect the health of the marine environment. Listing them all would require a separate book. A partial list of organizations is included, many of whom are international or national in scope and serve as umbrellas for regional organizations. On their websites you'll find links to those that operate locally and regionally. In that way you can find one close to home that you can support with your time, your knowledge and your financial resources.

The most important step you can take: Find an organization that matches your interests in boating and protection of the marine environment. Then join that organization.

Organizations

Concert for the Oceans
701 North 15th Street, 2nd Floor, St. Louis, MO 63103
www.cfto.org
Established to create better awareness about ocean conservation and climate change.

Coral Reef Alliance
417 Montgomery Street, Suite 205, San Francisco, CA
(415) 834-0900, www.coralreefalliance.org
Working for the preservation of coral reefs.

Georgia Strait Alliance
195 Commercial St., Nanaimo, BC V9R 5G5
(250) 753-3459; Fax: (250) 753-2567
e-mail:gsa@georgiastrait.org

Greenpeace
702 H Street NW, Suite 300, Washington, DC 20001
(800) 326-0959, www.greenpeace.org
Long-time organization working for the protection of the oceans.

Intergovernmental Oceanographic Commission: www.ioc.unesco.org
This part of UNESCO provides UN member states with a mechanism for cooperation on ocean study and policy. Maintains OceanPortal, which features an extensive list of regional organizations working to protect the marine environment.
www.iode.org/oceanportal

Marine Environmental Education Foundation
Larry Innis, Chairman
529 Bay Dale Ct., Arnold, MD 21012
(877) 892-0011 Fax (248) 541-2689, E-mail: meef@meef.org
www.meef.org
Sponsors of the National Clean Boating Campaign

Ocean Futures Society
325 Chapala Street, Santa Barbara, CA 93101
(805) 899-8899, www.oceanfutures.org
The organization founded and directed by Jean-Michel Cousteau.

Oceans Alive
257 Park Avenue South, New York, NY 10010
www.oceansalive.org

People for Puget Sound
911 Western Avenue, Suite 580, Seattle, WA 98104
(206) 382-7007,
people@pugetsound.org, www.pugetsound.org
A non-profit group working to protect and restore the health of
Puget Sound and the Northwest Straits through education and
action.

Pew Institute for Ocean Science
126 East 56th Street, New York, NY 10022
www.pewoceanscience.org

Save Our Seas
P.O. Box 813 Hanalei, HI 96714, (808) 651-3452
www.saveourseas.org
An international organization working to preserve, protect and
restore the world's oceans for future generations.

The Marine Mammal Center
1065 Fort Cronkhite, Sausalito, CA 94965
(415) 289-7335, www.marinemammalcenter.org
Operating throughout California to rehabilitate, protect and educate
about marine mammals.

US Environmental Protection Agency (EPA)
Ariel Rios Building, 1200 Pennsylvania Avenue NW,
Washington, DC 20460
(202) 272-0167, www.epa.gov

Waterkeeper Alliance
50 S. Buckhout, Suite 302, Irvington, New York 10533
(914) 674-0622, info1@waterkeeper.org, www.waterkeeper.org
Coordinates more than 100 Riverkeeper, Coast, Bay, Sound, Inlet,
Cape, Channel, Creek and Shore Keepers programs around the world.
For a searchable list of waterkeeper programs, or to start your own,
visit their website.

World Ocean Network
Sainte-Beuve - Bp 189, 62203 Boulogne-Sur-Mer Cedex, France
(+33) (0)3 21 30 99 99 Fax (+33) (0)3 21 30 93 94
E-mail: info@worldoceannetwork.org
Sponsors of the annual World Ocean Day on June 8.

Pass Along Your Boat Green Tips

Got a boating tip that's beneficial to the environment?

Boating is one of the oldest forms of transportation, and over the thousands of years that humans have been boating, many different problems and challenges have been encountered and solved. Sometimes old solutions that were beneficial to the environment have been forgotten by most boaters — like the fishermen during World War II who realized they could run their diesels on vegetable oil (see section on biodiesel), or the mariners who put cayenne pepper in bottom paint to make it a more effective anti-fouling agent (see section on bottom painting). Sometimes just plain old human ingenuity forces us to come up with solutions to boating problems that turn out to have positive environmental consequences, like the boaters who made crankcase breathers from used plastic water containers, or the scientist who discovered a way of releasing hydrogen peroxide in bottom paint as an anti-fouling agent.

If you've got a boating tip that's good for the maintenance or operation of your boat and also beneficial for the environment, please share it with other boaters. Help spread the word that good boating can be good for the environment.

Steps You Can Take

- Go to the Ecomarine Institute website, www.ecomarine.org, and click on "Share Your Boat Green Tip." There you can let others know about what you've discovered, or what information you think is missing from this book.

- Ask your marina or port authority to place your boat green tip in the next issue of their newsletter.
- Make an announcement at your next yacht club or boating association meeting.
- Drop an e-mail to a local organization working to protect the marine environment. They're always looking for positive steps that others can take, and they'll help spread your thoughts and ideas to others.
- Inform your local Coast Guard station, Coast Guard Auxiliary or Power Squadron.
- If your idea involves boating laws and regulations, contact the applicable state organization that handles boating regulation and enforcement and let them know.
- If your idea involves a piece of equipment or a system on your boat, contact the equipment manufacturer and let them know.
- If your idea involves development of a piece of equipment, don't be afraid to write it up in detail and consider getting a patent for it. There's no reason why a great idea shouldn't be patented and rewarded. ePaint, the company that makes environmentally sound bottom paint, has many patents for the processes that it uses.
- Use your boat as a demonstration project of your idea. Other boaters are always looking for boating solutions that work. Before biodiesel was popular, I filled up my tank with 100% homemade biodiesel for our annual summer cruise up the Inside Passage. I didn't have to tell people about what fuel I was burning; they smelled it and flocked to ask me about biodiesel.
- Don't be surprised if your ideas and interests turn you into a local resource. When people recognize your commitment to boating and to the environment, they'll seek out your opinion.

Endnotes

Chapter 2

1. "There Must Be Something in the Water." Press release, *Discover Boating* [online]. [Cited May 15, 2007]. discoverboating.com/info/pressrelease.aspx?id=15170

Chapter 3

1. *America's Living Oceans: Charting a Course for Sea Change*. Pew Oceans Commission. Arlington, VA. 2003

2. A. Knap, et al. "Indicators of Ocean Health and Human Health: Developing a Research and Monitoring Framework." *Environ Health Perspect*, *110*, pp. 839-845, 2002.

3. C.D. Harvell, et al. "Climate Warming and Disease Risks for Terrestrial and Marine Biota." *Science*, *296*, pp. 2158-2162, 2002.

4. R.A. Myers and B. Worm. "Rapid Worldwide Depletion of Predatory Fish Communities." *Nature*, *423*, pp. 280-283, 2003.

Chapter 4

1. Many facts cited come from "America's Wetlands: A Vital Link Between Land and Water." Environmental Protection Agency. Washington, DC.

2. Tom Vanden Brook. "Raw Human Sewage Pouring into America's Lakes and Streams." *USA Today*, August, 20, 2002.

3. Ibid.

4. Ibid.

5. "Wadeable Streams Assessment: A Collaborative Survey of the Nation's Streams." Environmental Protection Agency. Washington, DC, 2006.

Chapter 6

1. Garrett Hardin. "The Tragedy of the Commons." *Science*, *162*, pp. 1243-1248, 1968.

2. The Clearwater Organization. 112 Little Market St. Poughkeepsie, NY 12601845-454-7673: www.clearwater.org.

Chapter 10

1. "Stop the Drop" a campaign by the BOAT US Foundation. See the website: www.boatus.com/foundation/cleanwater/drops/FuelTips.asp

Chapter 11

1. Information compiled in part from "How to Make an Oil Spill Kit." New Hampshire Department of Environmental Services. Concord, New Hampshire.

Chapter 13

1. David Pimentel and Tad Patzek. "Ethanol Production Using Corn, Switchgrass, and Wood; "Biodiesel Production Using Soybean and Sunflower." *Natural Resources Research*, *14*, 1, pp. 65-76, 2005.

2. Alexei Barrionuevo. "It's Corn vs. Soybeans in a Biofuels Debate." *New York Times*, July 13, 2006. A summary and report on study done by the National Academy of Sciences.
3. Ibid.
4. "Issues with Ethanol As an Additive in Non-Road Motor Fuel." Presentation by John W. McNight at the International Boatbuilders Exposition (IBEX) Conference [online]. [Cited May 15, 2007]. 2006.
  www.nmma.org/lib/docs/nmma/gr/environmental/mcknight_Ethanol.ppt

Chapter 15
1. David Tether. "The Electric Wheel: Horsepower and Motors, or Apples and Oranges." *Mulithull Magazine*, May/June 2001.

Chapter 16
1. From the West Marine Catalog [online]. [Cited May 15, 2007].
  www.westmarine.com/webapp/wcs/stores/servlet/westadvisor/10001/-1/10001/headandholdingtank.htm

Chapter 30
1. Some of these steps are taken from the booklet, "Brightwork: A Best Management Practices Manual for Maine's Boatyards and Marinas" [online]. [Cited May 15, 2007]. Maine Department of Environmental Protection.
  www.maine.gov/dep/blwq/docwatershed/marina/bmp.htm.

Chapter 31
1. Joseph E. Costa. "A Review of the Performance of Bilge Socks Proposed for use in Buzzards Bay Recreational Boats." Dartmouth, MA, 2000.

Chapter 32
1. C.J. Loretto and S.V. Proud. *Effects of TBT on Dogwhelks at Marine Inlets and Marinas.* Fifth interim report of the Marine Conservation Society survey of dogwhelk populations around the UK. Report PECD/7/8/186, Marine Conservation Society, Ross-on-Wye, 1993.
2. K. Kannan et al. "Butyltin Residues in Southern Sea Otters (Enhydra lutris nereis) Found Dead Along California Coastal Waters." *Environ. Sci. Technol.*, 32 , pp. 1169-1175, 1998.
3. J. Santos-Saachi et. al. "On Membrane Motor Activity and Chloride Flux in the Outer Hair Cell: Lessons Learned from the Environmental Toxin Tributyltin." *Biophysical Journal*, 88, pp. 2350-2362, 2005.

Chapter 33
1. Federal Trade Commission, "Guides for the Use of Environmental Claims." Washington, DC.

Chapter 35
1. "Clean Marinas, Clear Values." US EPA. EPA 841-R-96-003. Washington, DC, August 1996.

Chapter 37
1. These guidelines were developed by the Whale Museum of Friday Harbor, WA.
2. These guidelines developed by the Florida Conservation Organization and Save the Manatee.

Chapter 38
1. Some of these steps from Anne Cameron Siegal, "Ahoy, Fluffy. How to Keep Pets Safely Afloat." *Washington Post*, E1, July 7, 2002.

Chapter 45
1. "Clean Marinas, Clear Values." US EPA. EPA 841-R-96-003. Washington, DC, August 1996.
2. National Oceanic and Atmospheric Administration, Office of Coastal Management [online]. [Cited May 15, 2007]. coastalmanagement.noaa.gov/marinas.html

Index

regulations. *See* coast guard; *acts by name*
resins, 66, 91, 92, 150
rivers, 11, 15, 17. *See also* Clearwater organization; inland waters

About the Author

Clyde W. Ford is an author and avid boater. He's the former vice president of WAKE, the Whatcom Association of Kayak Enthusiasts, and a former kayak instructor and guide for the Whatcom County Department of Parks and Recreation. Along with his partner, Chara Stuart, Clyde has cruised the Inside Passage on their 30-foot Willard trawler, *Mystic Voyager,* powered by biodiesel.

Clyde writes articles on boating safety for *PassageMaker Magazine* and is the editor of the Books and Boats Blog at the magazine's website. He's also published both nonfiction and fiction including books on health and mythology and a series of contemporary nautical thrillers entitled the "Charlie Noble Novels," set along the Inside Passage. The winner of numerous literary awards, Clyde received the prestigious Hurston-Wright legacy award in 2006 for his east coast novel, *The Long Mile.*

A sought-after public speaker and frequent presenter at boat shows and boating groups, Clyde's also made appearances on the Oprah Winfrey Show and National Public Radio to discuss his writing and his work.

If you have enjoyed *Boat Green* you might also enjoy other

BOOKS TO BUILD A NEW SOCIETY

Our books provide positive solutions for people
who want to make a difference. We specialize in:

Sustainable Living • Conscientious Commerce • Environment and Economy
Ecological Design and Planning • Natural Building & Appropriate Technology
Educational and Parenting Resources • Health & Wellness
Progressive Leadership • Resistance and Community

New Society Publishers

ENVIRONMENTAL BENEFITS STATEMENT

New Society Publishers has chosen to produce this book on Enviro 100, recycled paper made with **100% post consumer waste**, processed chlorine free, and old growth free.

For every 5,000 books printed, New Society saves the following resources:[1]

26	Trees
2,377	Pounds of Solid Waste
2,616	Gallons of Water
3,412	Kilowatt Hours of Electricity
4,322	Pounds of Greenhouse Gases
19	Pounds of HAPs, VOCs, and AOX Combined
7	Cubic Yards of Landfill Space

[1]Environmental benefits are calculated based on research done by the Environmental Defense Fund and other members of the Paper Task Force who study the environmental impacts of the paper industry.

For a full list of NSP's titles, please call **1-800-567-6772** *or check out our website at:*

www.newsociety.com

NEW SOCIETY PUBLISHERS